Amish Gardening All Year Long: How to Thrive, Strive, and Survive Using Amish Secrets

Bradford M. Smith

Copyright © 2025 Bradford M. Smith

All Rights Reserved.

ISBN: 9798311039994

Table of Contents

Chapter 1: Introduction to Amish Gardening

Chapter 2: The Amish Garden: What You Need to Know

Chapter 3: Sowing the Seeds: Amish Gardening Techniques

Chapter 4: Amish Canning: Preserving the Harvest

Chapter 5: Amish Recipes for the Garden

Chapter 6: Winter Gardening: How to Grow Even in the Coldest Months

Chapter 7: The Amish Pantry: The Key to Year-Round Freshness

Chapter 8: Amish Lore and Gardening Traditions

Chapter 9: Safety and Cleaning in Amish Gardens

Chapter 10: The Future of Amish Gardening: Preserving Tradition in a Modern World

Appendix 1: Tools and Resources

Appendix 2: Seasonal Gardening Calendar

Appendix 3: Growing Heirloom Varieties

Appendix 4: Harvesting and Preservation Charts

Appendix 5: Amish Gardening Techniques and Processes

Glossary

References

About the Author

Chapter 1: Introduction to Amish Gardening

Overview: Introduction to Amish Culture and Its Connection to Nature

The Amish are a distinct group within the larger Anabaptist tradition, known for their commitment to simplicity, humility, and strong religious beliefs. Their lifestyle, built on deep-rooted traditions, places a significant emphasis on farming, gardening, and living harmoniously with nature. While they are perhaps best known for their rejection of modern technology, what often goes unnoticed is their exceptional ability to cultivate and sustain life through their farming practices.

This chapter explores the Amish approach to gardening, which embodies the principles of sustainability, simplicity, and community. It will delve into their philosophy, gardening techniques, and ways in which they manage their gardens throughout the year. We will see how their connection to nature, their self-reliant lifestyle, and their community-driven practices come together to create a gardening system that has flourished for centuries.

The Amish Way of Life: History and Values

To understand Amish gardening, it's essential to first grasp the way of life that shapes it. The Amish are a religious group that originated in Europe during the late 17th century, led by Jacob Amman. They were a part of the Anabaptist movement, which believed in adult baptism, separation from the world, and non-violence. Early Amish settlers, seeking religious freedom and the ability to practice their faith in peace, emigrated to America, primarily settling in Pennsylvania, Ohio, and Indiana.

The Amish lifestyle is governed by a set of religious beliefs and traditions that emphasize separation from the broader society, called the "English." Amish communities avoid most modern technologies such as electricity, automobiles, and telephones, as they believe these can lead to pride, greed, and distractions from religious devotion. Instead, they embrace a simpler, more self-sufficient lifestyle.

Central to this lifestyle is farming and gardening. For the Amish, the land is a sacred gift from God, and taking care of it is an act of stewardship. By living close to nature, the Amish foster a profound respect for the earth and all it provides. It is through this relationship with the land that gardening has become not just a livelihood, but a way of life.

The Amish also value strong family and community bonds, and gardening is often a communal activity. Families work together to plant, harvest, preserve, and share their crops. These traditions have been passed down from generation to generation and continue to shape the Amish experience.

The Importance of Gardening: How It Ties into Amish Life

Gardening is at the heart of the Amish experience, and it serves several important purposes. First and foremost, it is a means of self-sufficiency. The Amish grow much of their own food, from vegetables and fruits to herbs and grains. This not only ensures that they are providing for their families, but it also reduces dependence on outside sources. The Amish live by the principle of "independence," believing that they should provide for themselves as much as possible.

Additionally, gardening provides an opportunity for the Amish to connect with nature. For many, it is a spiritual practice. The rhythm of planting, tending, and harvesting aligns with the natural rhythms of life, and the work is often seen as an expression of faith. For the Amish, caring for their gardens is an act of stewardship that honors God's creation.

Moreover, gardening plays a significant role in the Amish economy. Many Amish communities sell surplus crops and homemade products, such as jams, preserves, and baked goods, at local markets. This helps sustain their families and communities, allowing them to live with minimal interaction with the outside world.

Beyond practical and economic reasons, gardening is also a source of pleasure and fulfillment. The process of growing plants from seed to harvest is deeply satisfying, and many Amish families take great pride in their gardens. The colorful vegetables, the fragrance of fresh herbs, and the abundance of fruits and flowers bring joy to their lives and create a sense of pride in their work.

The Key Principles of Amish Gardening

Amish gardening is built on several key principles that distinguish it from modern, industrialized farming techniques. These principles focus on sustainability, organic practices, and deep respect for the land. They are rooted in the values of simplicity, community, and faith. Some of the key principles of Amish gardening include:

1. **Simplicity**: The Amish embrace a simple life, and this extends to their gardening practices. They avoid modern chemical fertilizers and pesticides, opting instead for natural methods of soil enrichment and pest control. For example, Amish gardeners often use compost, animal manure, and crop rotation to maintain soil health.
2. **Sustainability**: Amish gardens are built to be sustainable. The emphasis is on producing food in a way that doesn't deplete the land. This means using methods that are kind to the soil, preserve its fertility, and minimize waste. Crop rotation, companion planting, and the use of organic fertilizers are key components of sustainable Amish gardening.
3. **Self-Sufficiency**: Growing their own food is essential to the Amish lifestyle. Not only does this provide a steady food supply for families, but it also ensures that the Amish are not dependent on outside sources. This commitment to self-sufficiency extends beyond food and includes building their own homes, making their own clothing, and crafting their own furniture.
4. **Faith and Stewardship**: The Amish believe that the earth is a gift from God, and gardening is seen as an act of stewardship. By caring for the land and nurturing its bounty, they fulfill their responsibility to God and the community. Gardening is viewed as a spiritual practice that connects the Amish to the natural world and to their Creator.
5. **Community**: Gardening is not just an individual activity; it is a community effort. Amish families often share seeds, tools, and knowledge, and they help one another with planting, harvesting, and preserving the harvest. This communal approach fosters a

sense of cooperation and mutual support, which is at the heart of Amish life.

What Makes Amish Gardening Different: A Comparison to Modern Methods

At first glance, Amish gardening may seem old-fashioned or outdated, especially in contrast to modern, industrialized farming methods. However, when we take a closer look, we find that Amish gardening is incredibly effective, efficient, and environmentally sustainable.

One of the key differences between Amish gardening and modern methods is the absence of synthetic fertilizers and pesticides. Instead, Amish gardeners rely on organic methods such as composting, crop rotation, and companion planting to enrich the soil and protect plants from pests. This approach not only reduces the environmental impact of gardening but also leads to healthier, more nutrient-dense food.

Another distinction is the use of manual labor instead of machinery. While industrial farms rely on tractors, harvesters, and other machines, Amish gardeners use hand tools, such as hoes, rakes, and shovels, to plant, maintain, and harvest their crops. This approach may be more labor-intensive, but it ensures that gardening remains a deeply personal and hands-on experience.

Additionally, Amish gardens tend to be smaller and more diverse than modern farms. Rather than focusing on a few large crops, Amish gardeners grow a wide variety of vegetables, fruits, herbs, and flowers. This diversity not only helps maintain a balanced and healthy diet but also supports biodiversity and prevents the depletion of the soil.

Lastly, Amish gardeners prioritize sustainability and self-sufficiency. They aim to create a garden that provides all the food their family needs, with enough surplus to share with others. This contrasts with industrial farming, which often focuses on maximizing profits and yields, sometimes at the expense of the environment and the health of the land.

Conclusion

The Amish way of life and their approach to gardening are deeply intertwined. Gardening is not just a means of survival for the Amish—it is a way of life, an expression of faith, and a symbol of their commitment to simplicity, sustainability, and community. Through their gardening practices, the Amish honor the land, preserve their traditions, and provide for their families and communities. In the following chapters, we will explore the techniques, traditions, and secrets that make Amish gardening so effective, and learn how we can apply these methods to our own lives to thrive, strive, and survive all year long.

Chapter 2: The Amish Garden: What You Need to Know

Introduction to Amish Gardening

When you first step into an Amish garden, you might notice something that sets it apart from the typical suburban backyard: simplicity, order, and harmony with nature. Amish gardens are not sprawling, overly manicured landscapes but are practical, efficient, and beautiful in their own right. Amish gardeners work the land as a means to provide for themselves and their families, and in doing so, they have cultivated practices that have stood the test of time.

This chapter will explore what makes an Amish garden truly unique, the key principles Amish gardeners follow, and what you need to know if you wish to replicate these time-honored techniques in your own garden. From understanding soil preparation and planting techniques to knowing the best crops for an Amish garden, this chapter is your first step toward mastering the art of Amish gardening.

Amish Garden Design: Simplicity and Functionality

One of the most notable features of Amish gardening is its design, which prioritizes function over form. Amish gardens are practical, organized spaces designed to grow a wide variety of food crops that will feed the family throughout the year. At first glance, Amish gardens might appear modest or even plain, but they are, in fact, highly efficient and built to meet the family's specific needs.

Creating the Garden Plot

Amish gardens are typically located near the home, making it easier to tend to them regularly. Unlike large commercial farms, Amish garden plots are generally compact, and families work with the space available to them. The size of the garden will vary depending on the family's needs, but most Amish gardens are large enough to provide for the family's food needs with some extra to sell or trade within the community.

The garden plot is often square or rectangular, with neat rows of crops organized in a grid-like fashion. This method maximizes space and allows for efficient planting, maintenance, and harvesting. Every inch of soil is utilized, and no space goes to waste. When designing an Amish garden, efficiency is paramount. Paths between rows are kept narrow, while the growing area itself is maximized.

Companion Planting and Crop Rotation

One of the fundamental principles in Amish gardening is the use of companion planting and crop rotation. Companion planting involves planting specific plants next to one another that benefit each other, whether by enhancing growth, deterring pests, or improving soil health. For example, planting basil next to tomatoes can help repel harmful insects, while marigolds are known to keep away nematodes that can harm the roots of other plants.

Crop rotation is another key practice. Growing the same crops in the same soil year after year can deplete the soil of nutrients, leading to poor yields. Amish gardeners are keenly aware of the importance of rotating crops to keep the soil healthy. By changing the types of crops planted in each area of the garden each season, Amish gardeners help ensure that the soil remains rich in nutrients and free from disease.

Soil Preparation: Building the Foundation for a Thriving Garden

Soil preparation is one of the most critical elements of Amish gardening. Without healthy soil, plants cannot thrive, and the entire gardening effort can be compromised. Amish gardeners take great care in preparing their soil, using natural methods to improve its structure, fertility, and health.

Amish Soil Amendments

Instead of using synthetic fertilizers, the Amish rely on organic methods to improve soil health. One of the most common soil amendments used by the Amish is compost. Composting is the process of breaking down organic matter, such as vegetable scraps, yard waste, and animal manure, into nutrient-rich soil. The Amish create their compost piles using kitchen scraps, leaves, grass clippings, and manure from their livestock, such as cows, chickens, and horses.

Manure is highly valued in Amish gardening, as it contains vital nutrients like nitrogen, phosphorus, and potassium, which are essential for plant growth. The Amish also use a mix of composted manure and other organic materials to create a rich, fertile environment for their crops.

In addition to compost, Amish gardeners often use cover crops to improve soil quality. Cover crops, such as clover or rye, are planted between main growing seasons to prevent soil erosion, suppress weeds, and add organic matter to the soil when they are tilled back in.

Amish Tilling Methods

Before planting, Amish gardeners till their soil to loosen it and ensure that it's aerated properly. This is typically done using hand tools, such as hoes, spades, and forks, or, in larger gardens, with horse-drawn plows. Amish gardening tends to avoid heavy machinery, which can compact the soil and disturb its natural ecosystem. Tilling by hand or with a horse-drawn plow allows for a gentler, more natural process of soil aeration.

Once the soil is prepared, Amish gardeners pay close attention to its texture, checking for signs of compaction or dryness. Amish gardens are often mulched to help retain moisture in the soil, preventing it from drying out during hot summer months.

The Planting Process: From Seed to Harvest

When it comes to planting, Amish gardeners take great care to choose the best varieties of seeds, focusing on heirloom and non-GMO crops. These seeds are passed down from generation to generation, often kept in small, carefully labeled envelopes, each containing a collection of seeds for a specific crop.

Seed Starting

Amish families generally start seeds indoors in the late winter or early spring. This allows for an earlier planting season when the weather warms up. The Amish often use simple, homemade containers for seed starting, such as wooden boxes or reused jars. They fill these containers with rich, organic soil or compost and carefully sow the seeds.

Unlike modern gardeners who may rely on plastic trays or cell packs, the Amish tend to favor natural, biodegradable materials. For example, they may use old newspaper or cardboard tubes to create homemade pots, which can be directly planted into the soil without needing to be removed.

Timing and Planting

Amish gardeners are attuned to the rhythm of the seasons and are careful to plant crops at the right time to ensure they grow properly. They follow traditional planting calendars based on local climate patterns, ensuring that crops are planted after the last frost in the spring and before the first frost in the fall.

In addition to timing, the Amish pay close attention to the moon phases when planning their planting schedule. Many Amish gardeners believe that planting according to the lunar cycle can lead to better yields. They observe the waxing and waning of the moon and adjust their planting dates accordingly.

Watering and Irrigation

Watering is an essential part of Amish gardening, and the Amish approach it with the same care and attention they give to all aspects of their gardening. While modern irrigation systems are often automated, Amish gardeners rely on simple, manual methods. Watering is done by hand, either with watering cans or with irrigation pipes that are gravity-fed, often using water from nearby wells or streams.

Rainwater harvesting is also a common practice. Many Amish families use rain barrels to collect water from their roofs, storing it for use during dry spells. This practice not only conserves water but also reduces the need for external water sources.

The Amish Approach to Pest Control

Pest control is a critical concern in any garden, but the Amish take a natural, holistic approach to dealing with pests. Instead of relying on chemical pesticides, they use a variety of organic methods to protect their crops.

Natural Pest Repellents

The Amish are known for using natural remedies to ward off pests. For example, they may plant aromatic herbs like basil, garlic, and mint near vulnerable crops to deter insects. Marigolds are often planted to keep pests such as aphids and nematodes at bay.

Additionally, the Amish may use homemade sprays made from natural ingredients like soap, hot pepper, and garlic to discourage pests. These sprays are applied directly to the leaves of plants and are safe for both the plants and the environment.

Beneficial Insects

The Amish are also careful to encourage beneficial insects in their gardens. Ladybugs, for example, are excellent natural predators of aphids, while bees are essential for pollination. Amish gardeners avoid using pesticides that could harm these helpful insects, understanding their vital role in the health of the garden.

Harvesting: Timing and Methods

When the time comes to harvest, Amish gardeners are meticulous in how they approach the task. Harvesting is done by hand, with care taken not to damage the plants or the fruits and vegetables. Amish gardeners understand that timing is crucial—harvesting too early or too late can impact the flavor, texture, and nutritional value of the crops.

Amish gardeners typically harvest crops in the morning when temperatures are cooler and the plants are less stressed. They use simple tools, such as knives, shears, and baskets, to carefully collect their produce. Many Amish communities also take the time to preserve their harvest through canning, drying, or freezing.

Conclusion

The Amish approach to gardening is grounded in tradition, faith, and sustainability. Their gardens are designed to provide for their families and communities, with an emphasis on efficiency, organic practices, and a deep respect for the land. Amish gardeners use techniques that have been passed down for generations, focusing on soil health, crop rotation, and natural pest control. Their gardens are a reflection of their values—simplicity, self-sufficiency, and stewardship of the earth.

As we move forward in this book, we will explore more specific techniques and tips that you can incorporate into your own garden, inspired by the wisdom of Amish gardeners. Whether you're growing vegetables for your family or embarking on a larger gardening project, the Amish approach offers valuable insights into how to create a thriving, sustainable garden all year long.

Chapter 3: Sowing the Seeds: Amish Gardening Techniques

Introduction: The Seeds of Tradition

When we think of gardening, we often picture rows of vegetables, neatly spaced and well-maintained, waiting to be harvested. For the Amish, gardening is much more than just growing food; it is a centuries-old tradition that reflects their deep connection to the earth and their commitment to self-sufficiency, simplicity, and sustainability. At the heart of Amish gardening is the practice of sowing the seeds—the act of planting, nurturing, and tending to the crops that will provide food for the family.

This chapter will delve into the techniques that the Amish use to sow their seeds, from preparing the soil to choosing the right seeds, planting with intention, and caring for the crops as they grow. You will learn how Amish gardeners achieve success with their methods, many of which have been passed down through generations. Whether you're a beginner or an experienced gardener, you will find valuable insights in these time-honored practices that will help you thrive in your own garden.

Amish Seed Selection: Quality, Heirloom, and Diversity

One of the first steps in Amish gardening is selecting the right seeds. For the Amish, seed selection is not simply a matter of picking whatever is available at the local store; it is a thoughtful, intentional process that takes into account the unique needs of the family, the local climate, and the traditions of their community.

Heirloom Seeds: A Tradition of Quality

The Amish are known for their preference for heirloom seeds. Heirloom seeds are those that have been passed down through generations, often for hundreds of years. These seeds are open-pollinated, meaning they can be saved and replanted year after year without losing their genetic integrity.

Unlike hybrid seeds, which are often produced by crossbreeding two different plant varieties for specific traits, heirloom seeds retain their original characteristics. For the Amish, using heirloom seeds is about more than just producing high-quality crops; it is about preserving the past. These seeds represent a link to their ancestors, their communities, and their way of life.

Many Amish families have their own collections of heirloom seeds that they save from year to year. These seeds may be passed down from generation to generation, stored carefully in envelopes or small jars, and labeled with their names, planting instructions, and notes about the variety's history. Amish gardeners often take great pride in their seed collections, seeing them as a family treasure.

Selecting for Climate and Growing Conditions

When selecting seeds, Amish gardeners consider the local climate and growing conditions. Amish communities are spread across the United States, from Pennsylvania to Ohio to Indiana, and each region has its own unique growing challenges. For example, gardeners in the colder northern regions will select seeds for hardier crops, such as root vegetables and cold-weather greens, while those in the warmer southern regions may choose crops like tomatoes, peppers, and melons.

Amish gardeners take the time to research the varieties that will thrive in their specific area. They often rely on local knowledge passed down through generations, as well as community networks, to learn about the best-performing crops for their environment. The Amish value practicality, so they choose seeds that will yield the most food with the least effort. This might mean opting for early-maturing varieties, drought-resistant crops, or those that are particularly suited to the local soil and weather.

Diversity in the Garden: A Wide Range of Crops

Another hallmark of Amish gardening is the diversity of crops grown. Amish families do not focus on just one or two crops; instead, they plant a wide variety of vegetables, fruits, herbs, and flowers. This diversity serves several purposes.

First, growing a diverse range of crops ensures that the garden provides a balanced diet throughout the year. Amish gardens typically include a mix of leafy greens (such as lettuce, kale, and spinach), root vegetables (such as potatoes, carrots, and beets), fruits (like apples, strawberries, and raspberries), and herbs (such as basil, mint, and thyme). This variety ensures that the family has access to a broad spectrum of nutrients and flavors.

Second, planting diverse crops helps to reduce the risk of crop failure. If one crop is affected by pests, disease, or unfavorable weather conditions, the other crops may still thrive. This practice, known as "risk diversification," is a way to safeguard the food supply.

Finally, diversity in the garden supports biodiversity in the soil. Different plants have different root structures, water requirements, and nutrient needs, which can help balance the soil's ecosystem and improve its overall health.

Soil Preparation: Creating a Foundation for Healthy Growth

Before sowing the seeds, Amish gardeners devote significant time and attention to preparing the soil. Healthy, fertile soil is the foundation for a successful garden, and the Amish take great care in ensuring that their soil is rich in nutrients, well-aerated, and properly tilled.

Amish Soil Enrichment Techniques

The Amish use a variety of methods to enrich the soil naturally. These practices are based on the principles of organic gardening, which emphasizes the use of natural materials to improve soil health.

One of the primary soil amendments used by Amish gardeners is compost. Composting is the process of breaking down organic matter, such as kitchen scraps, yard waste, and animal manure, into nutrient-rich soil. Amish families often create large compost piles, which are turned regularly to ensure that the material decomposes evenly. The resulting compost is then added to the garden beds, providing essential nutrients to the soil and helping to improve its structure.

In addition to compost, Amish gardeners often use manure from their livestock. Manure from cows, chickens, and horses is highly prized for its rich nutrient content. Amish farmers use it to fertilize their gardens, either by spreading it directly on the soil or by composting it with other organic materials. The manure provides essential nitrogen, phosphorus, and potassium, which are vital for plant growth.

Another important practice is the use of cover crops. Cover crops, such as clover, rye, and buckwheat, are planted between growing seasons to protect and enrich the soil. These crops prevent soil erosion, improve soil structure, and add organic matter when they are tilled back into the ground.

Tilling and Aerating the Soil

Tilling is a crucial step in soil preparation, and Amish gardeners use hand tools or horse-drawn plows to till their garden beds. Tilling helps to break up compacted soil, allowing air, water, and nutrients to reach the plant roots more effectively. Amish gardeners take care not to over-till the soil, as this can lead to soil erosion and a loss of essential organic matter.

In addition to tilling, Amish gardeners often use a technique called "double digging," where the soil is loosened by digging two levels deep. This process helps improve soil aeration and drainage, ensuring that the roots have ample space to grow and develop.

Sowing the Seeds: The Art of Planting

Once the soil is prepared, it is time to sow the seeds. The act of planting is an intentional, thoughtful process for Amish gardeners, who follow specific methods to ensure that their crops grow strong and healthy.

Planting by Hand

While modern gardeners may use seeders or mechanical planters, the Amish plant their seeds by hand. This method allows for greater control over seed placement, ensuring that the seeds are spaced properly and planted at the correct depth. Amish gardeners often use simple tools, such as hoes or trowels, to make shallow furrows in the soil for their seeds.

Hand planting also allows Amish gardeners to maintain a personal connection with their crops. Each seed is planted with care, and the act of sowing is seen as a spiritual practice, a way to nurture life and honor the land. Amish gardeners believe that the health of the seeds is directly tied to the care and intention with which they are planted.

Planting with the Moon

Many Amish gardeners follow the lunar cycle when planting their crops. The belief that the moon influences plant growth is a centuries-old tradition that has been passed down through generations. According to this practice, the best time to plant is during the waxing moon, when the moon is moving from new to full. This phase is believed to promote strong root development and healthy growth.

In contrast, the waning moon, when the moon is moving from full to new, is seen as a time for harvesting or planting crops that grow underground, such as root vegetables. Amish gardeners often consult planting charts or almanacs to determine the optimal times for sowing seeds based on the moon's cycle.

Caring for the Garden: Ongoing Attention and Maintenance

Amish gardeners know that planting is just the beginning of the process. After the seeds are sown, the real work begins: tending to the plants, ensuring that they have the right conditions to grow, and protecting them from pests and disease.

Watering the Garden

Watering is a critical aspect of plant care. Amish gardeners rely on a combination of natural rainwater and manual watering methods. Many Amish families use rain barrels to collect water from the roof, which can be used to water the garden during dry spells.

Watering is typically done in the morning or evening to avoid the heat of the midday sun, which can cause the water to evaporate quickly. Amish gardeners often water at the base of the plants, avoiding overhead watering that can encourage fungal diseases.

Weed and Pest Control

Weeding is another essential task in Amish gardening. Weeds compete with crops for water, nutrients, and sunlight, so they must be kept in check. Amish gardeners often use hand tools, such as hoes or weeding forks, to carefully remove weeds from the soil. Mulching is another technique used to suppress weeds while also retaining moisture in the soil.

Pest control is handled with natural remedies, as discussed in Chapter 2. Amish gardeners use companion planting, beneficial insects, and homemade sprays to protect their crops from harmful pests. They also rotate crops regularly to reduce the likelihood of pest infestations.

Conclusion: The Fruits of Labor

Sowing the seeds is just the beginning of a long and rewarding journey. For Amish gardeners, the process is an act of faith, a way to honor the land and provide for their families. By selecting the right seeds, preparing the soil carefully, and following traditional planting methods, Amish gardeners ensure that their crops will thrive and provide sustenance for years to come.

In the following chapters, we will explore the ongoing maintenance of the garden, from harvesting to preserving the bounty of the season. The lessons learned from the Amish garden will inspire you to approach your own garden with the same care, intention, and respect for nature.

Chapter 4: Amish Canning: Preserving the Harvest

Introduction: The Art of Canning

For the Amish, food preservation is an integral part of their lifestyle. Canning is not merely a way to store food for the winter; it is a time-honored tradition that connects the community to their harvest, their ancestors, and the land. Canning represents the Amish philosophy of self-sufficiency, sustainability, and a deep respect for the cycles of nature. It allows families to preserve the bounty of their garden, ensuring a supply of wholesome, homegrown food year-round.

This chapter delves into the Amish tradition of canning, exploring its history, techniques, safety precautions, and the recipes that make it so essential to Amish life. We will also explore the nutritional benefits of canning and how Amish canning practices differ from modern methods. By the end of this chapter, you will have a solid understanding of how to can your own garden bounty, ensuring that you can enjoy the fruits of your labor long after the harvest season ends.

The History of Amish Canning: Preserving the Harvest for Generations

Canning has been a vital part of Amish culture for centuries. Before refrigeration and modern storage techniques, preserving food for the winter months was a necessity for survival. The Amish, who have always prioritized self-sufficiency and simplicity, embraced canning as a way to store the excess food they grew in their gardens, allowing them to provide for their families during the colder months when fresh produce was scarce.

Canning was traditionally done by hand, with Amish women spending hours over a hot stove, preparing and preserving fruits, vegetables, and meats. The process involved sterilizing jars, preparing the food, sealing the jars, and then processing them to ensure that the food would stay safe to eat for months or even years.

In the early days, Amish families relied on open-pit canning methods, where jars were heated directly in a pot of water over an open fire.

Today, many Amish communities use more modern equipment like stovetops and electric water-bath canners, but the principles of canning have remained largely unchanged. The Amish have always taken great pride in their canning practices, and it remains a cornerstone of their food culture.

The Importance of Canning in Amish Life

Canning serves several important purposes for the Amish. First and foremost, it ensures that families have a reliable food supply throughout the year. The Amish rely on their gardens to provide much of their food, but the growing season is limited. By canning, they are able to preserve the harvest, ensuring that they have access to fresh, wholesome food during the winter months when fresh produce is unavailable.

In addition to providing food security, canning is also a way for the Amish to honor the cycles of nature. The process of harvesting, preparing, and preserving food is a deeply spiritual practice for many Amish families. It is a way to give thanks for the abundance of the earth and to connect with the land and their ancestors.

Canning also allows Amish families to avoid dependence on store-bought goods. The Amish strive to live independently from the modern world, and canning provides a way for them to maintain control over their food supply. By preserving their own food, they are able to avoid the preservatives, chemicals, and artificial ingredients often found in commercially canned goods.

Finally, canning is a communal activity. Many Amish communities gather together to can, sharing their knowledge, expertise, and resources. This sense of community is central to Amish life, and canning serves as a way for families to come together and work toward a common goal.

Canning Equipment: Tools of the Trade

The tools and equipment used in Amish canning are simple yet effective. While the technology may have evolved over the years, the basic principles of canning have remained the same. Amish canning relies on a few essential tools that every canner should have on hand:

1. Canning Jars and Lids

The most essential items in the canning process are the jars themselves. Canning jars are typically made of glass and come in a variety of sizes, with pint, quart, and half-gallon jars being the most commonly used. Amish canners favor sturdy, reliable jars that can withstand the heat and pressure of the canning process.

Lids are another crucial component. Most canning jars require a two-piece lid system: a metal ring that holds the lid in place and a flat metal lid with a sealing compound. The sealing compound creates a vacuum seal that keeps the food fresh by preventing air from entering the jar. When the lid is properly sealed, it makes a popping sound, signaling that the jar has been successfully sealed.

2. Water-Bath Canner

The water-bath canner is used for high-acid foods such as fruits, jams, and pickles. It consists of a large pot with a rack inside to hold the jars. The jars are placed on the rack, and the pot is filled with water. The water is then brought to a boil, and the jars are processed in the boiling water for a set period of time, depending on the food being canned.

The Amish often use large, heavy-duty water-bath canners that can hold multiple jars at once. These canners are designed to distribute heat evenly, ensuring that the jars are processed at the right temperature.

3. Pressure Canner

For low-acid foods such as vegetables, meats, and soups, a pressure canner is necessary. The pressure canner works by trapping steam inside the pot, increasing the pressure and temperature to a level that kills harmful bacteria and ensures the food is safe to eat. The Amish often use manual pressure canners, which require careful monitoring to ensure that the correct pressure is maintained throughout the process.

Pressure canners are essential for preserving non-acidic foods, as they reach higher temperatures than a water-bath canner and are capable of destroying dangerous pathogens that can survive in low-acid environments.

4. Jar Lifter and Funnel

A jar lifter is a tool used to safely lift hot jars in and out of the canner. It is designed with long handles and rubber-coated ends to prevent burns. A funnel is used to fill jars with food, ensuring that the food is properly packed without spilling. The funnel is especially useful when canning liquids, such as juices or soups, as it prevents messes and spills.

5. Canning Kit

Many Amish canners use a complete canning kit, which includes essential tools such as a jar wrench, lid lifter, and magnetic lid wand. These tools make the canning process more efficient and ensure that the jars are properly sealed.

The Canning Process: Step-by-Step

The canning process is a precise and methodical one, and the Amish approach it with patience and care. The following is a step-by-step guide to the canning process, following the traditional methods used by the Amish:

Step 1: Prepare the Jars and Lids

The first step in the canning process is to prepare the jars and lids. Begin by washing the jars thoroughly with hot, soapy water to remove any dust or debris. After washing, sterilize the jars by placing them in a large pot of boiling water for 10 minutes. This ensures that the jars are free of bacteria and microorganisms that could spoil the food.

Next, prepare the lids. Place the flat metal lids in a separate pot of hot (but not boiling) water to soften the sealing compound. Do not boil the lids, as this can damage the sealing compound and cause the lid to fail to seal properly.

Step 2: Prepare the Food

While the jars and lids are being sterilized, prepare the food that will be canned. This can include fruits, vegetables, meats, or jams. Depending on the type of food, you may need to peel, chop, blanch, or cook it before canning.

For fruits, such as peaches or apples, the Amish typically peel, core, and slice the fruit before packing it into jars. Vegetables are often blanched (briefly boiled and then plunged into ice water) to preserve their color, texture, and nutritional value. Meats, such as chicken or beef, are usually cooked and cut into pieces before being packed into jars.

Step 3: Fill the Jars

Once the food is prepared, it's time to fill the jars. Place the food into the jars, leaving about ½ inch of headspace at the top of the jar. This allows for expansion during the canning process. If necessary, add water, syrup, or brine to cover the food. Be sure to pack the food tightly but not too tightly, as air bubbles can form and affect the seal.

Step 4: Seal the Jars

Place the prepared lids onto the jars and screw on the metal rings until they are finger-tight. Do not overtighten, as this can prevent the jars from sealing properly. Once the jars are sealed, they are ready to be processed.

Step 5: Process the Jars

The next step is to process the jars. For high-acid foods like fruits and pickles, use a water-bath canner. Fill the canner with water, ensuring that the jars are fully submerged. Bring the water to a boil, then process the jars for the appropriate amount of time, depending on the type of food.

For low-acid foods like vegetables and meats, use a pressure canner. Fill the canner with water, add the jars, and seal the lid. Bring the canner to the correct pressure, then process the jars for the required time.

Step 6: Cool and Check the Seal

Once the jars have been processed, remove them from the canner and place them on a clean towel to cool. As the jars cool, you should hear a "pop" sound, indicating that the seal has formed. Check the seals by pressing down in the center of the lid; if it doesn't pop back, the jar has sealed properly.

Once the jars have cooled completely, store them in a cool, dark place. Properly canned food can last for months, or even years, depending on the type of food and the canning method used.

Amish Canning Recipes: Traditional Favorites

Amish canning recipes are known for their simplicity and flavor. Below are a few traditional recipes that are staples in Amish homes:

1. Amish Sweet Pickles

- **Ingredients**: Cucumbers, sugar, vinegar, cloves, mustard seeds, cinnamon sticks.
- **Method**: Slice cucumbers and soak them in a saltwater brine for several hours. Prepare a syrup of vinegar, sugar, and spices. Pack the cucumbers into sterilized jars, pour the syrup over them, and process in a water-bath canner.

2. Amish Apple Butter

- **Ingredients**: Apples, sugar, cinnamon, cloves, and allspice.
- **Method**: Cook down apples until they are soft, then puree the mixture. Add sugar and spices, then cook further until the mixture thickens to a spreadable consistency. Can in jars using a water-bath canner.

3. Amish Canned Tomatoes

- **Ingredients**: Tomatoes, salt, lemon juice.

- **Method**: Peel and crush the tomatoes. Pack them into sterilized jars, add salt and lemon juice, and process in a water-bath canner.

Conclusion: Preserving the Past, Ensuring the Future

Canning is an essential part of Amish life and culture. It allows families to preserve the harvest, ensure food security, and maintain independence from the outside world. Amish canning practices are simple, time-tested, and rooted in a deep respect for the land and its bounty.

By adopting these practices in your own life, you can not only preserve the flavors of your garden but also create a sustainable, self-sufficient food supply that will provide nourishment for months to come. Whether you are canning fruits, vegetables, or meats, the principles of Amish canning will help you thrive, strive, and survive, just as they have for generations of Amish families.

Chapter 5: Amish Recipes for the Garden

Introduction: The Connection Between Gardening and Amish Recipes

One of the hallmarks of Amish life is a deep connection to the land, and this connection is reflected in the foods they grow, prepare, and enjoy. From hearty stews and savory casseroles to homemade jams and pickles, the Amish tradition of cooking is rooted in a reverence for homegrown ingredients. The act of gardening and the act of cooking are inseparable in Amish culture, as the garden serves as the source of nourishment for the family, and the kitchen transforms these garden harvests into delicious, wholesome meals.

In this chapter, we will explore a collection of Amish recipes, focusing on those that make use of the bounty harvested from the garden. These recipes highlight the Amish approach to food: simple, nourishing, and crafted with care. Through these recipes, we will see how Amish gardeners preserve the seasonal abundance of their gardens and bring it to the table in a way that sustains their families throughout the year.

We will cover a wide range of Amish recipes, including savory dishes, side dishes, desserts, and preserves, all of which are staples in Amish homes. These recipes are practical, flavorful, and steeped in tradition—just like the gardens that produce the ingredients.

Amish Vegetables: The Heart of the Garden

The heart of any Amish garden is the vegetables it produces. These vegetables are not only the foundation for many of the meals the Amish prepare, but they also play a key role in food preservation. Amish gardeners grow a variety of vegetables to ensure that there is always something fresh to eat, even when the growing season ends.

Let's explore some of the most common vegetables in the Amish garden and how they are used in Amish recipes.

1. Potatoes: The Staple Crop

Potatoes are a staple crop in Amish gardens, prized for their versatility, ease of cultivation, and ability to store well through the winter months.

The Amish use potatoes in a variety of dishes, from mashed potatoes to potato salad to casseroles.

Amish Mashed Potatoes

- **Ingredients**: Potatoes, butter, milk, salt, pepper.
- **Method**: Peel and boil the potatoes until tender. Mash them with butter, milk, salt, and pepper until smooth and creamy. For an extra touch of flavor, some Amish families add a little cream cheese or sour cream.

Potato and Onion Casserole

- **Ingredients**: Potatoes, onions, butter, cheese, breadcrumbs, salt, and pepper.
- **Method**: Slice the potatoes and onions, then layer them in a baking dish. Melt butter and pour it over the vegetables, and top with cheese and breadcrumbs. Bake until golden and bubbly.

2. Corn: A Sweet and Savory Treat

Corn is another beloved vegetable in Amish gardens. Whether it's sweet corn eaten fresh in the summer or preserved for the winter through canning or freezing, corn is an essential part of the Amish diet.

Amish Creamed Corn

- **Ingredients**: Fresh corn kernels, butter, heavy cream, sugar, salt, and pepper.
- **Method**: In a large pan, melt butter and sauté the corn kernels until tender. Add heavy cream, a bit of sugar, and season with salt and pepper. Cook until the mixture thickens to a creamy consistency.

Cornbread

- **Ingredients**: Cornmeal, flour, sugar, eggs, milk, baking powder, salt, and butter.
- **Method**: Mix together the dry ingredients, then whisk in the wet ingredients. Pour the batter into a greased baking dish and

bake until golden and firm. This sweet and hearty cornbread is the perfect accompaniment to any meal.

3. Tomatoes: The Flavor of Summer

Tomatoes are one of the most versatile vegetables grown in Amish gardens. They are used in everything from fresh salads to soups, sauces, and stews. Amish gardeners often grow heirloom varieties for their rich flavor and ability to be used for both fresh eating and canning.

Amish Fresh Tomato Salad

- **Ingredients**: Fresh tomatoes, cucumbers, onions, olive oil, vinegar, sugar, salt, and pepper.
- **Method**: Slice the tomatoes, cucumbers, and onions, then toss them together in a bowl. Combine olive oil, vinegar, sugar, salt, and pepper to make a dressing, then pour over the vegetables. Toss to combine and let marinate for at least an hour before serving.

Amish Spaghetti Sauce

- **Ingredients**: Fresh tomatoes, garlic, onions, basil, oregano, olive oil, salt, and pepper.
- **Method**: Sauté garlic and onions in olive oil until soft. Add chopped fresh tomatoes and cook down until thickened. Stir in fresh basil and oregano, season with salt and pepper, and simmer for about an hour. This sauce can be used immediately or canned for later use.

4. Carrots: Sweet and Nutritious

Carrots are a common vegetable in Amish gardens, known for their sweetness and versatility. Whether eaten raw, cooked, or preserved, carrots play an important role in the Amish kitchen.

Amish Glazed Carrots

- **Ingredients**: Fresh carrots, butter, honey, salt, and pepper.

- **Method**: Peel and slice the carrots, then boil them until tender. Melt butter in a skillet, then stir in honey, salt, and pepper. Toss the cooked carrots in the glaze and cook for a few more minutes to allow the flavors to meld.

Pickled Carrots

- **Ingredients**: Carrots, vinegar, sugar, garlic, dill, mustard seeds, salt, and water.
- **Method**: Slice the carrots into thin strips and pack them into jars. In a saucepan, combine vinegar, sugar, garlic, mustard seeds, and salt. Bring to a boil, then pour the hot brine over the carrots. Seal the jars and process in a water-bath canner.

Preserving the Garden: Canning and Freezing

In Amish culture, preserving the garden's bounty is just as important as harvesting it. Canning and freezing are common methods of preserving fruits and vegetables, ensuring that the family has access to fresh produce year-round. Below are some traditional Amish methods for preserving the harvest.

1. Canning Jams and Jellies

Amish families often make jams, jellies, and preserves from their fruit harvest. These sweet spreads are not only enjoyed on bread and biscuits but also make excellent gifts for family and friends.

Amish Strawberry Jam

- **Ingredients**: Fresh strawberries, sugar, pectin, lemon juice.
- **Method**: Crush the strawberries and mix with sugar and lemon juice. Bring to a boil, then add pectin and cook until thickened. Ladle into sterilized jars and process in a water-bath canner.

Amish Peach Jam

- **Ingredients**: Fresh peaches, sugar, pectin, lemon juice.

- **Method**: Peel and chop the peaches, then combine with sugar and lemon juice. Boil the mixture until it thickens, then add pectin and cook for a few more minutes. Pour into jars and seal.

2. Freezing Vegetables

In addition to canning, the Amish also freeze vegetables to preserve their freshness. Freezing is an easy and efficient way to store excess produce, especially for vegetables like corn, beans, and peas.

Amish Freezer Corn

- **Ingredients**: Fresh corn on the cob, butter, salt.
- **Method**: Blanch the corn by boiling it briefly in water, then cool it in an ice bath. Cut the kernels from the cob and toss them with melted butter and salt. Pack the corn into freezer bags and store in the freezer.

Amish Freezer Beans

- **Ingredients**: Fresh green beans, salt.
- **Method**: Trim the beans and blanch them in boiling water for several minutes. After cooling, pack the beans into freezer bags and season with salt. Store in the freezer for later use.

Amish Desserts: Sweet Treats from the Garden

In Amish kitchens, desserts are a cherished part of every meal. Often made with fresh fruits and vegetables from the garden, these desserts are simple but delicious.

1. Amish Apple Crisp

- **Ingredients**: Apples, sugar, flour, oats, butter, cinnamon, salt.
- **Method**: Slice the apples and place them in a baking dish. Mix the remaining ingredients to form a crumbly topping, then sprinkle it over the apples. Bake until the apples are tender and the topping is golden brown.

2. Amish Pumpkin Pie

- **Ingredients**: Fresh pumpkin, sugar, cinnamon, cloves, ginger, eggs, cream, pie crust.
- **Method**: Roast the pumpkin, then puree it and mix with sugar, spices, eggs, and cream. Pour the mixture into a prepared pie crust and bake until set. This warm, spiced pie is perfect for fall.

Conclusion: Bringing the Garden to the Table

The Amish way of cooking is a reflection of their deep connection to the land. Through their gardens, they grow the ingredients that form the foundation of their meals—simple, hearty dishes made with love and care. Whether it's the sweetness of a summer tomato, the richness of a winter squash, or the comforting warmth of a bowl of mashed potatoes, Amish recipes bring the abundance of the garden to the table in a way that nourishes both body and soul.

In the following chapters, we will continue to explore how the Amish use their gardens to live sustainably throughout the year, from canning and preserving to preparing meals that make the most of the harvest. These recipes serve as a reminder that the food we grow and eat is not just sustenance; it is a reflection of our values, our traditions, and our connection to the earth.

Chapter 6: Winter Gardening: How to Grow Even in the Coldest Months

Introduction: Amish Winter Gardening – A Lifelong Tradition

In many parts of the world, the winter months mark a time of dormancy for gardens. With frost and snow covering the ground, it may seem as though gardening is impossible in the colder seasons. However, the Amish have long understood that with the right techniques, a garden can continue to thrive even during the coldest months of the year. Winter gardening is not just a way of extending the growing season, but a key component of the Amish lifestyle of self-sufficiency, sustainability, and resilience.

In this chapter, we will explore how the Amish approach winter gardening, focusing on techniques that allow them to grow fresh, healthy produce even in the depths of winter. From cold frames and greenhouses to indoor gardening and preservation methods, the Amish have developed practical strategies to ensure that their families are well-fed all year long. Whether you live in a northern climate with harsh winters or in a milder region, you will discover valuable insights and time-tested methods for winter gardening, inspired by the Amish.

The Amish Approach to Winter Gardening

Winter gardening might seem like an oxymoron, but for the Amish, it is a way of life. They approach winter gardening with the same principles of sustainability, resourcefulness, and care that they apply to their gardens throughout the rest of the year. Rather than viewing winter as a time of scarcity, the Amish see it as an opportunity to adapt and innovate.

For many Amish families, the garden is the heart of their food supply. Fresh produce is a cornerstone of their diet, and they are keenly aware that the winter months can bring a decrease in the availability of fresh food. The Amish rely on their gardens not just in the summer but throughout the year, including winter. By adapting their gardening methods, they ensure that their families can continue to enjoy homegrown vegetables and herbs, even when the snow is falling outside.

In order to achieve this, the Amish use a variety of techniques that protect plants from the cold while maximizing the growth of vegetables. These methods allow them to continue growing, harvesting, and eating fresh food even when the garden outside is covered in snow.

Techniques for Winter Gardening

There are several proven methods Amish gardeners use to extend the growing season and grow food in winter, all rooted in the idea of creating a protected, warmer microenvironment for the plants. Whether growing inside a structure or by using natural materials to shield crops, these techniques have been passed down through generations and are adapted to the needs of each particular region.

1. Cold Frames: A Simple Solution for Winter Growing

One of the most common methods used by the Amish to extend the growing season is the cold frame. A cold frame is essentially a miniature greenhouse that traps sunlight and retains heat, creating a warmer environment for plants. Cold frames are typically made from a wooden box structure with a glass or clear plastic lid to allow sunlight to enter. The box is placed directly on the soil, and the plants inside are protected from the harsh winter weather.

Cold frames are especially effective for growing hardy vegetables such as spinach, lettuce, kale, and carrots. These crops can tolerate some frost, but the cold frame provides enough warmth to keep them growing during the winter months. The Amish use cold frames to grow salad greens, root vegetables, and herbs, providing their families with fresh produce even when the outdoor garden is dormant.

The key to success with cold frames is to use them in the right location. The frame should be placed in a sunny spot with good exposure to direct sunlight. Amish gardeners typically place the cold frame on the south side of their homes or near a sheltered wall, where it will receive the most sunlight during the day. During particularly cold weather, Amish gardeners can use blankets, straw, or other materials to further insulate the cold frame and keep the plants warm.

2. Greenhouses: A More Controlled Environment

For those who want to grow more crops during the winter or need a more controlled environment, a greenhouse is a perfect solution. A greenhouse allows for year-round growing by creating a consistent, warm environment for plants. In Amish communities, greenhouses are often used not only for growing vegetables but also for starting seeds in the early spring and protecting delicate seedlings from late frosts.

Greenhouses can be built using a variety of materials, but Amish families typically construct their greenhouses from wood and plastic. The structure is usually unheated, relying on solar energy to warm the interior, though some families may use small, wood-burning stoves for additional heat during the coldest months.

Amish gardeners use their greenhouses to grow vegetables like tomatoes, peppers, herbs, and greens throughout the winter. The greenhouse protects the plants from the harsh winter winds and snow while allowing them to thrive in the warmer, more consistent temperatures inside. Like cold frames, greenhouses can be used to grow crops that are hardy and able to withstand frost, or they can be used to start seeds that will be transplanted into the garden in the spring.

3. Indoor Gardening: Growing in Small Spaces

In addition to cold frames and greenhouses, Amish families have also developed creative ways to grow food indoors during the winter. Indoor gardening is a great way to grow herbs, small vegetables, and microgreens even in small spaces. Amish families with limited land often rely on indoor gardening to supplement their food supply during the winter months.

Amish indoor gardening often involves using simple containers, such as pots, trays, or wooden boxes, to grow plants on windowsills, countertops, or in dedicated indoor garden spaces. Some Amish families use traditional methods of growing such as soil and water, while others use small hydroponic systems or self-watering containers to provide the right amount of nutrients and moisture to the plants.

The Amish often grow herbs like basil, parsley, thyme, and rosemary indoors during the winter. These herbs are used to flavor soups, stews, and other dishes, adding freshness and variety to the winter diet. In addition to herbs, vegetables such as lettuce, spinach, and radishes can be grown indoors. These plants do not require a lot of space, and their quick-growing nature makes them perfect for indoor gardening.

Indoor gardening is also a great way to teach children about gardening, as it can be done in small, manageable spaces. Amish families often involve their children in the growing process, helping them to plant, water, and care for the plants. This fosters a sense of responsibility and connection to the food they eat.

4. Row Covers: A Simple Yet Effective Method

For some Amish gardeners, row covers are a key tool for growing in the winter months. Row covers are lightweight fabrics that are placed over garden beds to protect plants from cold weather, frost, and snow. The covers allow sunlight to penetrate while trapping heat inside, creating a warmer environment for the plants.

Row covers are particularly useful for protecting crops like lettuce, spinach, kale, and other leafy greens that can survive a light frost but need some extra warmth to continue growing during the winter. The Amish use row covers to extend the growing season for these crops and to keep them growing even in colder temperatures.

Row covers are made from a variety of materials, including cloth, plastic, or specialized agricultural fabric. Amish gardeners prefer lightweight materials that allow for good airflow while providing sufficient protection from the elements. In addition to being used in winter, row covers are also used to protect plants from insects during the growing season.

5. Winterizing Your Garden: Preparing for the Cold

Even with the best techniques for winter gardening, it is essential to properly winterize your garden to ensure that it remains healthy and productive year after year. The Amish take great care in preparing their gardens for winter, as they know that the garden's health in the spring begins with how it is treated in the fall.

Winterizing a garden involves several key tasks, including:

1. **Clearing the Garden**: Remove any dead plants, weeds, and debris from the garden. This helps prevent the buildup of pests and diseases over the winter months.
2. **Mulching**: Apply a thick layer of mulch over the garden beds to protect the soil from freezing and to help retain moisture. Mulch also helps prevent weed growth in the spring.
3. **Composting**: The fall is a great time to add organic matter to the compost pile. Amish gardeners often use fallen leaves, vegetable scraps, and other plant material to create a rich, nutrient-filled compost that can be used to enrich the soil in the spring.
4. **Covering Perennials**: For perennial plants, the Amish use row covers or other protective coverings to shield them from the winter weather. This helps ensure that the plants will survive the cold and return in the spring.
5. **Preparing Tools**: Clean and sharpen garden tools to ensure that they are ready for use when the weather warms up. Amish gardeners take great care in maintaining their tools, as they are essential for maintaining a healthy garden.

Winter Harvesting and Preserving

For the Amish, winter gardening is not just about growing fresh produce; it is also about harvesting and preserving food for future use. Amish families rely on canning, freezing, and drying to preserve the harvest from their winter gardens.

Winter vegetables like carrots, parsnips, and cabbage can be harvested throughout the winter, providing fresh food even when the garden appears to be dormant. These vegetables are often stored in cool, dry places or preserved through canning to ensure a steady food supply.

Herbs grown indoors or in cold frames can also be harvested and preserved by drying or freezing. The Amish often preserve herbs for use in soups, stews, and other dishes, ensuring that they have flavorful seasonings year-round.

Conclusion: Thriving Through the Winter

Winter gardening is an essential part of Amish life. Through the use of cold frames, greenhouses, indoor gardening, row covers, and proper garden preparation, Amish families are able to continue growing fresh, nutritious food throughout the coldest months of the year. This practice not only ensures a steady food supply but also allows the Amish to maintain their connection to the land and their commitment to self-sufficiency.

By adopting these techniques and adapting them to your own gardening practices, you can extend your growing season and enjoy fresh, homegrown produce year-round. Winter gardening may require some extra effort and ingenuity, but the rewards are well worth it. Whether you are growing greens in a cold frame or enjoying fresh herbs on your windowsill, winter gardening offers a way to thrive, strive, and survive even in the coldest months of the year.

Chapter 7: The Amish Pantry: The Key to Year-Round Freshness

Introduction: The Heart of the Amish Home

In Amish households, the kitchen is the heart of the home, and the pantry is the cornerstone of a well-stocked and self-sufficient lifestyle. The pantry not only stores food but also serves as a symbol of preparedness, sustainability, and deep-rooted traditions that span generations. For the Amish, it is more than just a place to keep food; it is a vital part of their everyday life, providing nourishment, preserving the harvest, and maintaining their ties to the land and their values of simplicity and independence.

The Amish pantry is a reflection of their commitment to growing, preserving, and consuming what is produced within their community. It is a space filled with homemade preserves, canned vegetables, dried herbs, grains, and other homegrown products—each jar, jar, or container a reminder of the hard work and care invested in preparing it. This pantry enables families to thrive year-round, even when the fresh produce from the garden is no longer available.

This chapter will explore the Amish pantry and its essential role in Amish life. From creating a well-stocked pantry to understanding how to store, preserve, and use your pantry goods, you will learn how to integrate Amish pantry principles into your own life to maintain a sustainable, self-sufficient lifestyle.

The Importance of a Well-Stocked Pantry

The Amish have long valued self-sufficiency, and one of the primary ways they achieve this is through the creation and maintenance of a well-stocked pantry. Having a pantry full of preserved food is not only a practical way to ensure that the family has enough to eat during the off-seasons but also an expression of the Amish ideal of living off the land, free from reliance on the outside world. By preserving and storing food, the Amish avoid purchasing processed, store-bought products laden with preservatives, chemicals, and artificial ingredients.

A well-stocked pantry is a means of preparedness. It allows Amish families to be prepared for unexpected events such as a poor growing season, an economic downturn, or even the long winters that might limit their access to fresh food. In this way, the pantry becomes a safety net for the family, providing them with everything they need to survive and thrive during challenging times.

The pantry is also a place of abundance. A well-preserved harvest from the summer months can feed a family throughout the entire year, with jars of tomatoes, peaches, pickles, jams, and sauces lining the shelves. The Amish rely on the pantry not only to store vegetables and fruits from their garden but also to keep grains, beans, rice, flour, sugar, and other staples. With a well-organized and thoughtfully stocked pantry, families can access these ingredients year-round and prepare wholesome meals with ease.

What to Include in an Amish Pantry

An Amish pantry is not just a collection of food items; it is a carefully curated collection of ingredients and products that allow families to create nourishing meals from scratch. Amish pantries are typically stocked with homegrown and homemade items, but they may also include bulk dry goods like flour, sugar, and grains that can be purchased in large quantities. Below are the key components of an Amish pantry:

1. Canned Goods: Preserving the Harvest

Canning is one of the most important methods the Amish use to preserve the bounty of their garden. The pantry shelves are often lined with jars of canned vegetables, fruits, and jams. These foods are not only convenient but also provide essential nutrition during the winter months when fresh produce is unavailable.

Some of the most common canned goods in the Amish pantry include:

- **Vegetables**: Tomatoes, beans, corn, carrots, peas, and potatoes.
- **Fruits**: Apples, peaches, pears, strawberries, cherries, and plums.
- **Pickles and Relishes**: Cucumbers, beets, green beans, and sweet peppers.

- **Jams and Jellies**: Strawberry, blackberry, grape, and apricot jams, as well as fruit preserves.

Canning not only helps extend the shelf life of produce but also locks in the fresh flavors of the harvest. Amish gardeners often can their crops in small batches to ensure that they can access them throughout the year without overwhelming the pantry. The process of canning is done with great care, and each jar is sealed tightly to ensure the food remains safe and flavorful for months.

2. Dried Goods: Stocking Up for Winter

Drying is another important method for preserving food in Amish homes. Drying fruits, vegetables, and herbs helps to retain the food's nutritional value and flavor while reducing the need for refrigeration. Dried foods are lightweight, shelf-stable, and easy to store in the pantry, making them ideal for the long winter months when access to fresh food is limited.

Common dried foods in the Amish pantry include:

- **Fruits**: Apples, peaches, apricots, and raisins.
- **Vegetables**: Tomatoes, green beans, peas, carrots, and corn.
- **Herbs**: Basil, thyme, rosemary, sage, mint, and oregano.

The process of drying food is simple but requires patience and attention. For example, Amish families often dry fruits and vegetables using dehydrators, hanging them in the sun, or even using wood stoves during the colder months to help speed up the drying process.

3. Grains, Beans, and Legumes: The Backbone of Amish Meals

Grains and legumes form the backbone of many Amish meals. Whether it's a hearty bowl of oatmeal in the morning or a comforting bean soup for dinner, these pantry staples provide the essential nutrients needed to sustain the family.

Some of the most common grains and beans found in the Amish pantry include:

- **Flour**: Wheat, cornmeal, and rye flour for baking bread, pies, and other baked goods.
- **Rice**: White, brown, and wild rice are used in a variety of dishes.
- **Beans**: Lima beans, kidney beans, navy beans, black beans, and pinto beans.
- **Oats**: Rolled oats and steel-cut oats are used for breakfast and baking.

Many Amish families mill their own flour, grinding grain at home to make fresh, nutritious flour for baking. This is often done with a hand-powered grain mill, which is powered by muscle or water, rather than electricity. Freshly ground flour is a staple in Amish baking and allows families to make everything from bread to muffins to pastries with ease.

4. Canning and Preserving Supplies: Stocking Up on Essentials

In addition to the food itself, an Amish pantry is stocked with the supplies needed to preserve food. Canning jars, lids, and rings are essential for canning vegetables and fruits, while vacuum-sealed bags are used for preserving meat, fish, and even some vegetables. Amish families also keep jars of homemade spices, herbs, and seasonings that are needed for preserving or enhancing dishes.

Organizing the Amish Pantry: Keeping It Tidy and Accessible

For the Amish, organization is key to a well-functioning pantry. The pantry should be easily accessible, with everything stored in a way that makes sense and is easy to find. Amish families use wooden shelves, baskets, and crates to keep their pantry neat and tidy, with jars stacked neatly and labeled with the contents and date of preservation.

A key principle in Amish pantry organization is rotating the stock. Older jars of canned goods are used first, and new jars are placed at the back of the shelf. This ensures that nothing goes to waste and that families always have access to fresh, preserved food.

Amish pantries are also organized by category, with jars of fruits, vegetables, pickles, jams, and herbs kept separately for easy identification. Grains, beans, and dry goods are often stored in large bins or barrels, keeping them fresh and easy to use.

Using the Amish Pantry: Making the Most of What You Have

Once the pantry is stocked, it is essential to use its contents wisely. The Amish are known for their resourcefulness, and they make the most of every item in their pantry, ensuring that nothing goes to waste. Here are some ways the Amish incorporate their pantry goods into their daily meals:

1. Amish Baking: A Pantry-Based Tradition

Baking is a central part of Amish life, and the pantry plays a crucial role in providing the necessary ingredients. With grains, flour, sugar, and other staples, the Amish are able to bake fresh bread, pies, cakes, cookies, and pastries from scratch.

Amish families often bake bread daily, making loaves of hearty, homemade bread to accompany meals. Common types of bread include white, whole wheat, rye, and cornbread. Freshly baked bread is served with butter, jams, or preserves from the pantry, creating a satisfying and nourishing meal.

2. Hearty Soups and Stews: Using What's on Hand

Soups and stews are a staple of the Amish diet, particularly during the colder months. A pantry stocked with dried beans, canned vegetables, and herbs makes it easy to whip up a hearty, nutritious meal. Amish families often make large batches of soup, allowing for easy leftovers that can be enjoyed throughout the week.

Common soup ingredients include beans, potatoes, carrots, onions, and garlic—often combined with homemade broth or stock from the pantry. Amish vegetable soups and stews are a great way to use preserved vegetables and create a comforting, wholesome meal.

3. Pickling and Preserving: Extending the Life of Produce

The Amish are known for their pickling skills, and the pantry is full of jars of pickled vegetables and fruits. These preserved goods are often used as condiments, side dishes, or main courses. Pickled cucumbers, beets, and onions are common in the Amish pantry, as are pickled peppers and carrots.

The act of pickling is not just a method of preserving; it's also a way to enhance the flavors of seasonal produce. With the right spices and brines, pickled vegetables can add a zesty, tangy kick to any meal.

Conclusion: Living with the Seasons, Year-Round Freshness

The Amish pantry is a living testament to the importance of self-sufficiency, sustainability, and community. It is a space where families come together to preserve the harvest, ensuring that they have access to wholesome, homegrown food all year long. Through canning, drying, and storing, the Amish create a pantry filled with nutritious foods that nourish the body, mind, and soul.

By adopting the principles of the Amish pantry, you can live more sustainably, make the most of your harvest, and provide your family with fresh, homegrown food throughout the year. Whether you're growing a small backyard garden or working with a larger plot of land, the Amish pantry offers a model for creating a well-stocked, resourceful, and nourishing food supply that will help you thrive in any season.

Chapter 8: Amish Lore and Gardening Traditions

Introduction: A Connection to Nature Through Storytelling

The Amish way of life is deeply intertwined with nature, and their relationship with the land extends far beyond the practical aspects of gardening and farming. For the Amish, the act of gardening is often rooted in cultural lore, religious beliefs, and stories that are passed down from generation to generation. These stories and traditions offer more than just practical advice; they are part of the cultural fabric that ties the community together, providing wisdom, guidance, and spiritual meaning in the work of growing food.

In this chapter, we will explore the lore and traditions that influence Amish gardening practices. From the symbolism of specific plants to the spiritual significance of seasonal rhythms, Amish gardening is not merely a physical act of planting and harvesting—it is a sacred practice that honors God's creation. We will also look at how storytelling and family traditions enhance the connection between the Amish and their gardens, fostering a deeper understanding of the land and its cycles.

Amish Gardening Traditions: Learning from the Land

Amish gardening traditions are often handed down through families, with each generation learning the methods and principles that have been practiced for hundreds of years. These traditions are passed along not only through instruction but also through storytelling, which helps to reinforce the cultural and spiritual connections between the Amish people and the land. Amish gardeners grow more than just food—they grow a deep connection to the earth, and through their work, they honor their faith, ancestors, and community.

1. The Cycle of Seasons: Planting with Purpose

In Amish culture, the changing of the seasons is seen as a reflection of life's spiritual cycles. The Amish are keenly attuned to the rhythms of the natural world, and their gardening practices are deeply influenced by the cycles of nature. For many Amish gardeners, the planting and harvesting of crops follow a rhythm that mirrors the cycles of life: sowing in the spring, nurturing throughout the summer, and harvesting in the fall. Winter, when the garden lies dormant, is seen as a time for rest, renewal, and reflection.

Amish gardeners believe that each season holds its own spiritual lessons. The act of planting seeds in the spring is viewed as an act of faith—just as a farmer plants a seed with the hope that it will grow, the Amish believe they must sow faith in God and trust that the harvest will come. Similarly, the harvest in the fall is a time for gratitude, as the community comes together to give thanks for the bounty that God has provided.

2. Garden Symbols: Plants and Their Meaning

Many Amish gardeners imbue their plants with symbolic meaning. Certain plants are chosen not only for their usefulness in the kitchen but also for their spiritual significance. The Amish view the garden as a living expression of God's creation, and each plant is thought to hold its own unique qualities.

- **Sunflowers**: A common sight in Amish gardens, sunflowers symbolize faith, loyalty, and the joy of creation. The Amish believe that sunflowers turn toward the sun, much like people should turn toward God for guidance and strength.
- **Lavender**: Known for its calming fragrance, lavender is often planted by Amish gardeners for its medicinal properties as well as its symbolic meaning of peace and purity. It is believed to bring tranquility and harmony to the home.
- **Pumpkins**: Pumpkins are not only a delicious fall vegetable but also symbolize abundance, prosperity, and the importance of providing for one's family. The act of growing pumpkins is viewed as a way of ensuring a bountiful harvest and a successful year.

These symbolic plants are often incorporated into the gardens as a way to honor both the practical and spiritual aspects of gardening. For the Amish, tending to these plants is a reminder of their connection to God and their commitment to living in harmony with nature.

Amish Stories and Folklore: The Wisdom of the Ancestors

Storytelling is an essential part of Amish culture, and many of the gardening traditions are passed down through stories and anecdotes shared by elders. These stories often contain lessons about life, nature, and faith, and they serve as a way to teach younger generations the importance of maintaining a strong connection to the land. Amish gardening folklore is rich in symbolism, offering valuable insights into how the Amish view the world and their role in it.

1. The Story of the Garden's First Seed

One popular Amish story tells of the very first seed planted in a garden. The tale speaks of a humble farmer who, upon receiving a handful of seeds, planted them in his garden with great care. As the plants grew, so did his understanding of the importance of patience, hard work, and faith. The story teaches that while gardeners may work hard to plant and care for their crops, it is ultimately God who provides the increase, and success is rooted in trust and gratitude.

This story is often shared among Amish families during planting season, serving as a reminder that gardening is not just a labor of love but also an act of faith. The moral of the story encourages patience and perseverance, and it underscores the idea that the harvest is a gift from God, earned through faith and diligence.

2. The Legend of the Healing Herb

Another popular story in Amish folklore involves a medicinal herb that was believed to have healing properties. According to the story, an elder in the community discovered the herb while walking through the woods. It was said that the plant could cure ailments and heal wounds. Over time, the herb became a cherished part of Amish gardens, and the story of its discovery was passed down through generations.

The story emphasizes the connection between the Amish people and nature, illustrating how the land can provide not only for physical needs but also for spiritual and emotional well-being. It also reinforces the idea that knowledge of plants and herbs is a sacred responsibility, passed down through generations to preserve both the health of the community and its traditions.

3. The Tale of the Cursed Garden

One of the more cautionary tales in Amish gardening folklore is the story of the "cursed garden." This story tells of a farmer who, after neglecting his garden and failing to tend to the soil, experienced poor harvests year after year. The story is often used to teach the importance of hard work, respect for the land, and the need to take care of one's crops. It serves as a reminder that gardening is not just about planting seeds—it is about nurturing and caring for the earth and working in harmony with it.

The tale of the cursed garden is often shared with younger generations to help them understand the responsibility of gardening. It teaches that the work is not always easy, but that it is worth the effort and that care and respect for the land are necessary for a fruitful harvest.

Gardening and Spirituality: Tending to the Soul

For the Amish, gardening is not just a practical task—it is also a spiritual practice. Many Amish believe that working the land is a way of serving God, and they approach gardening with reverence, treating the land as sacred. The act of planting, nurturing, and harvesting is seen as a form of stewardship, an offering to God that reflects the values of humility, gratitude, and faith.

1. The Garden as a Reflection of Faith

The Amish view their gardens as a reflection of their faith. Just as they believe that their lives should be a reflection of God's will, they believe that their gardens should reflect the beauty and order of creation. Amish gardens are often designed with care and intention, following principles of simplicity, orderliness, and harmony. These gardens are seen as a place where the Amish can connect with God, meditate on His creation, and reflect on their role in the world.

The Amish also believe that working the land is a way of honoring God's creation. They see the act of planting and harvesting as a way of fulfilling their responsibility as stewards of the earth. This sense of responsibility is deeply spiritual, and many Amish gardeners approach their work with reverence, seeing it as an opportunity to give thanks for the abundance of the land and to offer their efforts as a service to God.

2. The Cycle of Life in the Garden

The changing seasons are often viewed as a reflection of the cycle of life. In the spring, gardeners plant the seeds of new life, just as new beginnings are celebrated in the Amish community. The summer months bring growth and abundance, symbolizing the fulfillment of life's potential. The fall represents the harvest, a time of gratitude and reflection, while the winter symbolizes rest, renewal, and reflection—an opportunity to prepare for the next cycle.

In this way, Amish gardening is not only a seasonal practice but a spiritual journey that mirrors the larger cycle of life. Amish families often reflect on these cycles during the planting, growing, and harvesting seasons, contemplating the lessons that nature offers and finding spiritual meaning in the work of their hands.

The Future of Amish Gardening Traditions

While the core principles of Amish gardening remain unchanged, modern challenges and opportunities are beginning to influence how Amish communities approach gardening. Advances in sustainable farming techniques, new methods of preserving food, and changing climates all present new opportunities and challenges for the Amish gardener.

1. Adapting to Climate Change

As climate change brings more unpredictable weather patterns and extremes, Amish gardeners must find new ways to adapt. Some Amish communities have begun experimenting with water conservation methods, more efficient irrigation systems, and new types of crops that can withstand extreme weather conditions.

However, despite these changes, the Amish remain committed to their traditions of organic farming and sustainable gardening. Their commitment to living in harmony with the land means that they will continue to adapt to the changing climate in ways that preserve their values of stewardship and sustainability.

2. Passing Down Knowledge to Future Generations

The future of Amish gardening depends on the continued transmission of knowledge and traditions to younger generations. The Amish place great value on education and mentoring, and many older gardeners pass down their wisdom to the younger generation through hands-on training, storytelling, and shared experiences.

By teaching children and young adults the importance of gardening and the spiritual connections to the land, the Amish ensure that their gardening practices will continue for generations to come. The next generation of Amish gardeners will carry forward the wisdom and traditions of their ancestors, continuing the cycle of faith, stewardship, and sustainability.

Conclusion: The Spiritual Garden

Amish gardening is much more than an agricultural practice—it is a spiritual journey, deeply rooted in tradition, faith, and community. Through stories, symbols, and rituals, Amish gardeners connect with the land, honor God's creation, and reflect on the cycles of life. Gardening is not just about growing food; it is about nurturing the soul, cultivating patience, and living in harmony with nature.

As we embrace the wisdom and traditions of Amish gardening, we can deepen our own connection to the earth and develop a greater appreciation for the beauty and abundance that nature provides. Whether we are planting seeds, harvesting crops, or simply tending to our gardens, we can find spiritual meaning in every step of the process, knowing that, just as the Amish have done for centuries, we are working in partnership with the land to nourish our bodies and souls.

Chapter 9: Safety and Cleaning in Amish Gardens

Introduction: Ensuring a Healthy, Sustainable Garden

The Amish way of life is rooted in simplicity, sustainability, and a deep respect for nature. As stewards of the land, they believe in cultivating a garden that is not only productive but also healthy and free from harmful chemicals. This commitment to organic gardening practices goes hand in hand with their principles of environmental stewardship and personal responsibility. As gardeners, they ensure that every step of the process, from soil preparation to harvesting, is carried out with care for the environment and a focus on long-term sustainability.

However, maintaining a garden that thrives requires more than just planting seeds and letting them grow. Proper safety measures, as well as regular cleaning and maintenance, are essential to ensuring that the garden remains a safe and productive space throughout the year. This chapter will explore the importance of safety and cleanliness in Amish gardening, with a particular focus on the methods they use to create a healthy environment for both plants and gardeners.

We will delve into Amish approaches to safe gardening practices, including organic pest control, safe handling of tools and equipment, and creating a hygienic environment for growing food. Additionally, we will explore how Amish gardeners maintain clean spaces for food preparation and storage, ensuring that the food they grow remains safe, nutritious, and free from contaminants.

The Importance of Safety in the Amish Garden

In the Amish community, safety is not just a practical concern; it is an integral part of their values. The Amish believe that God has entrusted them with the responsibility of caring for the land, and that includes ensuring the health and well-being of both the plants and the people who tend to them. Therefore, safety in the garden is taken seriously, whether it involves using safe gardening tools, managing potential hazards, or protecting the garden from harmful pests and diseases.

1. Safe Use of Gardening Tools

One of the most basic but essential aspects of gardening safety is the proper use and maintenance of tools. Amish gardeners use a variety of hand tools for planting, weeding, and harvesting. These tools are typically simple and manual, reflecting the Amish commitment to avoiding modern technology. However, even with basic tools, proper handling and maintenance are essential to avoid accidents and ensure that tools remain functional and effective.

Tool Maintenance and Safety
Amish gardeners place great importance on maintaining their tools. A well-maintained tool is safer to use, lasts longer, and performs more effectively. Amish families often spend time each year cleaning, sharpening, and oiling their tools, ensuring that they are in good working condition. Regular maintenance helps prevent accidents, such as a dull knife slipping while harvesting vegetables or a rusted hoe breaking mid-use.

Amish gardeners also adhere to specific safety practices when using tools. For example, when using a hoe or rake, they ensure that the handle is firm and free from splinters, and they hold the tool at a proper angle to avoid strain on the body. Amish gardeners are also taught to use the right tool for the job, ensuring that they avoid unnecessary strain or injury.

Children and Tools
In Amish culture, children are often involved in gardening from an early age, and teaching them proper safety practices is a priority. Amish parents teach their children to handle tools responsibly, starting with small, child-friendly tools and gradually advancing to larger tools as they grow. This hands-on approach to gardening education emphasizes safety and respect for the tools.

2. Protecting the Garden from Pests and Diseases

Organic pest control is a cornerstone of Amish gardening. The Amish are committed to maintaining healthy, thriving gardens without the use of synthetic pesticides or chemical fertilizers. Instead, they use a variety of natural methods to prevent pest infestations and protect their crops from disease.

Companion Planting

One of the most common natural pest control methods used by Amish gardeners is companion planting. By planting certain crops next to each other, gardeners can naturally repel harmful insects and promote healthy growth. For example, planting marigolds with tomatoes can help deter aphids, while basil planted near peppers can repel mosquitoes and flies. Amish gardeners also use herbs like mint, rosemary, and garlic to naturally deter pests from their garden.

Beneficial Insects

Amish gardeners also welcome beneficial insects into their gardens. Ladybugs, for example, are natural predators of aphids and are encouraged in Amish gardens to help maintain a healthy balance. Bees are another important ally in the garden, as they help pollinate flowers and vegetables, ensuring a bountiful harvest. By creating an environment that attracts beneficial insects, Amish gardeners reduce the need for chemical pesticides while supporting biodiversity in their gardens.

Neem Oil and Other Organic Solutions

For more persistent pest problems, Amish gardeners may turn to organic solutions like neem oil, a natural insecticide that is safe for plants and the environment. Neem oil is effective against a wide range of pests, including aphids, caterpillars, and whiteflies, and it is often used in the Amish garden to maintain pest control without resorting to harmful chemicals.

Crop Rotation

Another key aspect of pest and disease management in Amish gardens is crop rotation. By changing the location of crops from year to year, gardeners prevent pests and diseases that target specific crops from becoming entrenched in the soil. This method not only helps control pests but also improves soil health by preventing nutrient depletion.

3. Creating a Safe Environment for Harvesting and Storage

The safety of harvested produce is just as important as its cultivation. The Amish are diligent about ensuring that the food they grow is clean, safe, and free from contamination. From proper harvesting techniques to storing food in clean conditions, the Amish take every precaution to ensure that their food remains healthy and free from harmful pathogens.

Harvesting Safely
When harvesting crops, Amish gardeners take care to use clean, sharp tools to avoid bruising or damaging the produce. Harvesting is often done early in the morning when the produce is cool, as this helps preserve its freshness and nutritional value. Amish gardeners also make sure to wash their hands thoroughly before handling produce, ensuring that the food remains free from contaminants.

Cleaning the Garden and Tools
After the harvest, Amish gardeners take the time to clean their tools, workspaces, and storage areas. Cleaning the tools after each use helps prevent the spread of diseases from plant to plant. Amish families also make sure that their storage areas are clean, dry, and free from pests to ensure that the harvested produce remains safe for consumption.

Canning and Preserving
Canning and preserving are key elements of Amish food storage. The Amish take great care in following proper canning procedures to ensure that their food is safely preserved for use during the winter months. Canning jars are sterilized before use, and each jar is carefully sealed to create a vacuum that prevents spoilage. Amish canning methods are simple and time-tested, relying on heat and sealing to preserve the food without the need for chemicals or artificial preservatives.

Cleaning the Garden: Keeping It Tidy and Productive

A clean garden is a productive garden, and the Amish understand that maintaining cleanliness in the garden is crucial to promoting plant health and ensuring a successful harvest. Regular cleaning helps to remove debris, prevent the spread of diseases, and create a space where plants can thrive.

1. Weeding and Mulching

Weeds are a constant challenge in the garden, but Amish gardeners use a variety of natural methods to keep them in check. Weeding is done by hand or with simple tools, ensuring that the weeds are removed without damaging the surrounding plants. Amish gardeners are diligent about weeding early and often, as this helps prevent weeds from taking root and competing with the crops for nutrients.

Mulching is another important part of garden cleanliness. By applying a layer of organic mulch—such as straw, leaves, or grass clippings—around the base of plants, Amish gardeners create a barrier that suppresses weed growth, retains moisture, and prevents soil erosion. Mulch also improves soil health as it decomposes, adding valuable organic matter to the soil.

2. Removing Dead Plant Material

At the end of each growing season, Amish gardeners carefully remove dead plant material from the garden. This includes spent plants, fallen leaves, and any other debris that could harbor pests or diseases. By cleaning up the garden in the fall, Amish gardeners prevent the buildup of harmful pathogens that could affect the crops in the following season.

Dead plants are often composted, creating nutrient-rich soil for future gardening. Amish families make sure to turn the compost regularly to ensure that it breaks down properly, adding valuable organic matter to the soil.

3. Sanitizing Tools and Equipment

Keeping gardening tools and equipment clean is essential for maintaining a healthy garden. Amish gardeners regularly clean their tools, removing dirt and plant matter that could harbor diseases. Tools are also sanitized with natural solutions, such as vinegar or a mild bleach solution, to prevent the spread of pathogens.

Equipment such as wheelbarrows, seed trays, and watering cans are cleaned thoroughly after each use, ensuring that they do not become breeding grounds for harmful bacteria or fungi.

The Amish Approach to Clean Living: Sustainable Practices for a Healthier Garden

Amish gardening goes hand in hand with their philosophy of clean, simple living. From using natural pest control methods to growing food without harmful chemicals, the Amish embrace practices that are good for the land, the body, and the soul. Their approach to cleanliness in the garden is not just about maintaining a tidy space; it is about fostering a relationship with the earth that promotes sustainability, health, and well-being.

1. Sustainable Practices: Composting and Recycling

The Amish practice composting to reduce waste and improve soil health. Composting allows them to recycle organic matter, such as vegetable scraps, leaves, and manure, and turn it into nutrient-rich soil. This practice not only reduces the need for synthetic fertilizers but also helps improve the overall health of the garden.

Composting is an ongoing process in Amish gardens, and families often have multiple compost bins or piles in various stages of decomposition. The compost is used to enrich the soil in the garden, providing the necessary nutrients for healthy plant growth.

2. Water Conservation

Water conservation is another important aspect of Amish gardening. The Amish use rain barrels and other water-saving methods to collect and store rainwater for use in their gardens. By conserving water, they reduce their dependence on external water sources and minimize waste.

Amish gardeners also take care to water their plants efficiently. Instead of using sprinklers that waste water, they often use drip irrigation systems or water directly at the base of the plants, ensuring that the water goes where it is needed most.

Conclusion: Creating a Clean, Safe, and Sustainable Garden

For the Amish, gardening is a sacred practice, and they take great care to ensure that their gardens remain healthy, clean, and productive. Through their focus on safety, cleanliness, and sustainability, Amish gardeners create spaces where plants can thrive without relying on harmful chemicals or artificial additives.

By adopting the Amish approach to safety and cleanliness in your own garden, you can cultivate a space that is not only beautiful and productive but also healthy and sustainable. Whether you are using organic methods to control pests, practicing good tool maintenance, or cleaning your garden at the end of the season, the principles of Amish gardening will help you create a garden that nourishes both the body and the soul.

Chapter 10: The Future of Amish Gardening: Preserving Tradition in a Modern World

Introduction: Tradition Meets Modernity

For centuries, the Amish have cultivated their gardens with a deep respect for tradition, guided by values of simplicity, sustainability, and faith. Their farming practices, which prioritize organic methods and self-sufficiency, have remained relatively unchanged over the years. Yet, as the world around them continues to evolve, so too must the Amish way of gardening adapt to meet new challenges. The future of Amish gardening lies at the intersection of preserving time-honored traditions and responding to the realities of the modern world, including climate change, evolving agricultural technologies, and a growing interest in sustainable farming practices.

In this chapter, we will explore the future of Amish gardening, examining how the Amish approach modernization while staying true to their core values. We will delve into the ways in which they are adapting to current environmental challenges, the growing interest in organic farming, and the increasing recognition of their gardening methods as models for sustainable agriculture. Furthermore, we will consider how Amish gardening practices might evolve in the coming decades and the role they will play in the future of food production.

The Core Values of Amish Gardening

Before exploring the future, it is essential to understand the core values that define Amish gardening. These values are rooted in their religious beliefs and cultural traditions, and they shape every aspect of their relationship with the land. They include:

1. Simplicity

At the heart of Amish gardening is the principle of simplicity. The Amish live in a world of reduced distractions, focusing on what is essential for a fulfilling life. This simplicity extends to their gardens, where they grow a variety of vegetables, fruits, and herbs using traditional, time-tested methods. The Amish reject modern conveniences like synthetic fertilizers, pesticides, and genetically modified organisms (GMOs), preferring instead to work with nature and respect its natural rhythms.

2. Self-Sufficiency

Self-sufficiency is a cornerstone of Amish life, and it is a key value that underpins their gardening practices. Amish families grow much of their own food, relying on their gardens to provide for their dietary needs year-round. From canning and preserving to growing a diverse range of crops, the Amish seek to minimize their reliance on external sources of food. This self-reliance is closely tied to their belief in being good stewards of the land.

3. Sustainability

Amish gardening practices emphasize sustainability, focusing on methods that preserve and enhance the land for future generations. They use organic practices like composting, crop rotation, and companion planting to ensure that their gardens remain fertile and healthy over the long term. This sustainable approach to farming minimizes the use of harmful chemicals and helps protect the environment for years to come.

4. Faith and Stewardship

Amish gardening is deeply connected to faith. For the Amish, gardening is not just about growing food; it is an expression of their belief in God and a way of serving Him. Gardening is seen as an act of stewardship, where they honor God's creation by caring for the land and the plants that grow on it. The cycles of planting and harvesting mirror their spiritual journey, reinforcing the idea that life is a series of seasons that require patience, faith, and dedication.

These core values have guided Amish gardening practices for centuries, and they will continue to shape the way the Amish engage with the land in the future. However, as new challenges arise, Amish gardeners are finding ways to adapt while remaining faithful to these principles.

Challenges Facing Amish Gardening

As with all farming practices, Amish gardening faces numerous challenges in the modern world. These challenges are often tied to broader environmental, economic, and societal shifts that have impacted farming communities everywhere. The Amish approach to gardening has allowed them to thrive despite these challenges, but the future of their gardening practices will depend on their ability to adapt to an evolving world.

1. Climate Change

One of the most pressing challenges facing Amish gardeners today is climate change. As global temperatures rise, weather patterns have become more unpredictable, with extreme weather events such as droughts, floods, and early frosts becoming more common. These changes are impacting the growing season, making it harder to predict when to plant, when to harvest, and how to protect crops from extreme conditions.

In response, Amish gardeners are increasingly turning to water conservation techniques, soil health practices, and resilient crop varieties to combat the effects of climate change. For example, some Amish gardeners are adopting mulching practices and drip irrigation systems to reduce water usage and conserve moisture in the soil. Others are experimenting with drought-resistant crops and focusing on hardy, early-maturing varieties that can withstand temperature fluctuations.

Additionally, some Amish communities are implementing techniques like windbreaks and shelterbelts—rows of trees or shrubs planted around gardens to protect crops from wind and extreme weather. These practices not only help prevent soil erosion but also create microclimates that provide additional protection for the plants.

2. Soil Depletion and Fertility

Soil fertility is another major challenge in modern agriculture, and it is one that the Amish have been addressing for generations through sustainable farming practices. However, with increasing demand for land and a growing global population, maintaining soil health and fertility has become more challenging.

The Amish have long relied on crop rotation, composting, and the use of organic fertilizers such as manure to maintain soil fertility. These methods help prevent soil depletion and ensure that the land remains productive over time. Moving forward, Amish gardeners will likely continue to rely on these techniques while incorporating new methods, such as no-till farming and the use of cover crops, to further improve soil health and reduce erosion.

3. Modernization and Technological Advancements

While the Amish are known for their rejection of modern technology, there is increasing interest in incorporating new, sustainable agricultural technologies into Amish farming practices. While the Amish remain steadfast in their commitment to simplicity and self-sufficiency, some Amish gardeners have found ways to incorporate environmentally friendly technologies into their gardens without compromising their values.

For example, some Amish gardeners are beginning to adopt solar-powered irrigation systems, which allow them to conserve water and reduce their reliance on external energy sources. Others are experimenting with more efficient greenhouse designs, using passive solar techniques to extend the growing season while minimizing energy consumption.

Despite these advancements, the Amish remain cautious about embracing technology. They are wary of becoming overly reliant on machines or technology that might compromise their connection to the land. As a result, their approach to modernization is typically one of careful consideration, ensuring that any new technology aligns with their values of simplicity, sustainability, and faith.

The Role of Amish Gardening in the Future of Sustainable Agriculture

As the world faces increasing environmental challenges, there is a growing interest in sustainable farming practices. Many of the techniques and principles used by Amish gardeners—such as organic farming, crop rotation, and soil conservation—are now being recognized as essential components of a sustainable food system. The future of Amish gardening is closely tied to the broader movement toward sustainable agriculture, and Amish gardeners have much to contribute to this global conversation.

1. Organic Farming as a Model for Sustainability

The Amish have been practicing organic farming long before it became a widespread trend. Their commitment to avoiding synthetic pesticides, herbicides, and chemical fertilizers aligns with the growing movement toward organic farming, which focuses on producing food in a way that is environmentally friendly and sustainable. In the future, Amish gardening methods will continue to serve as a model for organic farming, showing that it is possible to grow food without harming the environment or relying on harmful chemicals.

Amish gardening practices emphasize biodiversity, using diverse plantings to maintain healthy ecosystems and prevent pest outbreaks. By growing a variety of crops and using natural pest control methods, Amish gardeners help preserve biodiversity and protect the health of the soil. These practices are particularly important in a world where monoculture farming and the overuse of pesticides are leading to soil degradation and the loss of pollinators.

2. Local and Regional Food Systems

The Amish have long been advocates of local and regional food systems, growing food for their own consumption and selling surplus produce to local markets. This approach to food production helps strengthen local economies and reduces the carbon footprint associated with transporting food long distances. In the future, the Amish model of local food production will likely become even more relevant as communities seek to reduce their dependence on global supply chains and promote food security.

Amish gardeners are also increasingly sharing their knowledge with others, offering workshops, seminars, and mentoring programs to teach sustainable farming practices. This grassroots approach to education helps spread the message of sustainability and encourages others to adopt more eco-friendly gardening methods.

3. A Shift Toward Resilient Agriculture

As the climate continues to change, resilient agriculture will become increasingly important. The Amish have always been resilient farmers, adapting to changing conditions with practices that prioritize soil health, water conservation, and pest management. In the future, Amish gardening techniques will play a critical role in building resilient food systems that can withstand the challenges posed by climate change.

Resilient agriculture involves using farming methods that are adaptable to changing conditions and that prioritize long-term sustainability over short-term gains. Amish gardening practices, which focus on organic farming, conservation, and biodiversity, are a natural fit for this approach. As more farmers and gardeners look for ways to create food systems that can withstand extreme weather events and fluctuating conditions, the Amish model of gardening will become an increasingly important reference point.

Passing Down the Traditions: The Future of Amish Gardening

The future of Amish gardening lies in the hands of the next generation. Amish families place great importance on passing down their knowledge and traditions to their children, ensuring that the practices of their ancestors will continue for generations to come. This intergenerational transfer of knowledge is central to Amish life, and it ensures that their gardening methods will remain strong, relevant, and adaptable as the world changes.

Amish children are taught the basics of gardening from an early age, learning to plant seeds, care for plants, and harvest crops. They also learn the importance of organic farming, sustainability, and stewardship, values that will guide them throughout their lives. As the world continues to evolve, these values will remain constant, and the future of Amish gardening will be shaped by a commitment to faith, simplicity, and a deep respect for the land.

Conclusion: A Vision for the Future

The future of Amish gardening is bright, as it continues to offer a model of sustainability, self-sufficiency, and faith in a rapidly changing world. While the Amish remain rooted in tradition, they are also responding to the challenges of the modern world with creativity, resilience, and adaptability. By embracing sustainable practices, protecting the environment, and passing down their knowledge to future generations, Amish gardeners are ensuring that their practices will continue to thrive and inspire others for generations to come.

As the world looks for solutions to the challenges of climate change, food security, and sustainability, the Amish way of gardening offers a valuable lesson in how we can live in harmony with the land and build a better future for ourselves and our communities.

Appendix 1: Tools and Resources

A Buying Guide for Amish-Style Tools, Gardening Equipment, and Supplies

Gardening, especially Amish-style gardening, emphasizes the use of simple, effective tools that require little reliance on modern technology. Amish gardeners value tools that are built to last, offering durability, functionality, and efficiency. Many of these tools are handcrafted or produced by small-scale manufacturers, focusing on quality craftsmanship rather than mass production. In this section, we will explore Amish-style tools, gardening equipment, and supplies that align with their values of simplicity, sustainability, and self-sufficiency.

Whether you are just beginning to cultivate a garden, are looking to replace old tools, or want to incorporate Amish principles into your gardening methods, this guide will provide you with the essential tools and resources needed to tend to your garden with the same care and wisdom the Amish have used for generations.

Essential Amish-Style Gardening Tools

Amish gardening tools are known for their high quality, long-lasting durability, and simplicity of design. The following are the most important tools used by Amish gardeners and their corresponding uses:

1. Hand Tools: Simple, Durable, and Effective

Amish gardening often relies on manual tools to maintain efficiency without relying on technology or electricity. These tools are designed for precision, allowing gardeners to work the land by hand, often with greater care and less environmental impact.

- **Hoe**
  The hoe is one of the most basic yet essential tools in the Amish garden. Used for weeding, soil cultivation, and breaking up clods of soil, the hoe is available in various shapes and sizes. The traditional Amish hoe features a long, wooden handle and a

flat, sturdy metal blade that can be sharpened as needed. Look for a hoe with an ergonomic handle to reduce strain during extended use. Amish-made hoes are typically forged from high-quality steel and are built to last for many seasons of hard work.

- **Garden Rake**
  A garden rake is used to level soil, gather leaves, and smooth out soil beds for planting. Amish rakes often feature wide, durable tines made from steel or iron. The long wooden handle ensures good leverage while raking, which is critical for managing large plots. The Amish version of the rake emphasizes simplicity and balance, making it an essential tool for maintaining soil health.

- **Spade and Shovel**
  Spades and shovels are indispensable for digging, transferring soil, and breaking up hard ground. The Amish spade is often handcrafted with a straight blade and a strong wooden or metal handle. These spades are ideal for loosening soil, digging trenches, and planting deep-rooted crops like potatoes or carrots. Look for a spade that has a sharpened edge for ease of use and a comfortable grip.

- **Hand Fork (Cultivator)**
  The hand fork, also known as a cultivator, is a small but mighty tool used for loosening the soil, aerating it, and breaking up clumps. Amish hand forks are often constructed from steel, with four prongs designed to work through compacted soil. These hand tools are excellent for weeding, mixing in compost, and preparing small garden beds.

- **Pruning Shears**
  Pruning shears are essential for trimming plants, cutting back overgrown branches, and shaping bushes. Amish gardeners often use high-quality, hand-forged pruning shears made from steel that retains its sharpness over time. A well-maintained pair of shears can help keep your garden neat and healthy, preventing disease from spreading through improperly pruned plants.

2. Tools for Soil Preparation and Maintenance

The Amish take great care in preparing and maintaining their soil, ensuring it remains healthy and fertile throughout the seasons. Below are some specialized tools used to manage the soil:

- **Hand Tiller**
  A hand tiller is a small yet effective tool used for loosening the soil before planting. Amish-style hand tillers often feature a sturdy wooden handle and a set of rotating blades or tines. These tines help aerate the soil, making it easier for plant roots to penetrate the ground. For those with smaller garden plots or raised beds, the hand tiller is an ideal choice, as it provides greater control over the soil without using a large, motorized tool.
- **Broadfork**
  The broadfork is a tool used for deep tilling without disturbing the soil's structure. The Amish often use a broadfork for aerating garden beds and turning compost. A broadfork has several wide, curved tines that are inserted into the soil and then pulled up, loosening it without overturning it. This method helps maintain soil fertility and structure, preventing compaction and improving water retention.
- **Compost Aerator**
  The Amish prioritize composting to enrich the soil, and a compost aerator is a useful tool for turning and mixing compost piles. Compost aerators are designed with long handles and multiple tines or blades that help stir and oxygenate the compost. Aerating the compost ensures that it decomposes evenly and quickly, providing a nutrient-rich supplement to the garden soil.

3. Watering Tools: Natural and Efficient Systems

Water is vital for garden success, and Amish gardeners understand the importance of using water efficiently. While they avoid the use of modern irrigation systems powered by electricity, they use simple yet effective methods to ensure their plants get the moisture they need.

- **Rain Barrels**
  Rain barrels are an environmentally friendly way to collect and store rainwater for garden use. Amish gardeners often use large barrels or tanks made from food-grade plastic, metal, or wooden barrels to collect rainwater from roof gutters. This water can then be used for hand watering or gravity-fed irrigation systems, making it an efficient way to conserve water. Amish rain barrels are often fitted with a spigot for easy access to the water.
- **Watering Cans**
  Watering cans are a traditional tool used by Amish gardeners to water plants gently and evenly. Amish-style watering cans are usually made from galvanized steel, making them durable and rust-resistant. They are available in various sizes to accommodate different garden scales. Amish watering cans often have a long spout that allows for precision watering, reducing water wastage.
- **Drip Irrigation Kits**
  Although the Amish generally avoid high-tech systems, some are beginning to experiment with simple, hand-powered drip irrigation kits. These kits allow water to be delivered directly to the base of each plant, reducing water usage and minimizing evaporation. The Amish favor drip irrigation for its simplicity and efficiency, and many prefer to build their own systems using basic materials such as hoses, filters, and emitters.

4. Harvesting Tools: Collecting the Bounty

After months of care and nurturing, it's time to harvest the fruits of the Amish gardener's labor. The following tools make harvesting efficient and effective:

- **Harvesting Knife**
  A sharp, sturdy knife is an essential tool for harvesting vegetables and fruits. Amish gardeners typically use harvesting knives made from high-carbon steel that can be easily sharpened and maintained. The knives are ideal for cutting through tough stems, vines, and even roots. Look for a knife with a comfortable, ergonomic handle and a blade that holds its edge for extended use.

- **Basket or Harvest Tray**
  To collect the harvested produce, Amish gardeners often use baskets or trays made from woven wood, metal, or other natural materials. These baskets are light enough to carry through the garden while providing ample space to hold fruits, vegetables, and herbs without crushing them. Amish harvest baskets often feature handles for easy carrying and a sturdy construction that can withstand the demands of the harvest.
- **Scythe**
  For larger garden spaces, a scythe is a traditional tool used to cut tall grasses, weeds, or cover crops that have outgrown their space. Amish gardeners who work in larger fields or meadows may use a scythe with a long curved blade, designed for cutting with a sweeping motion. Scythes are often hand-forged with wooden handles and are highly effective for harvesting grains or cutting through dense vegetation.

Amish Gardening Supplies: Beyond Tools

In addition to essential tools, Amish gardeners rely on various supplies to help them tend to their gardens throughout the seasons. These supplies support their practices of organic gardening, sustainability, and food preservation.

1. Compost and Soil Amendments

- **Compost Bins**
  A compost bin or pile is essential for producing nutrient-rich compost, which is used to fertilize the soil. Amish gardeners often build compost bins out of wood or metal, creating simple, open-top bins that allow for easy turning and aeration of the compost. These bins can be built to various sizes, depending on the size of the garden and the volume of material to be composted.
- **Organic Fertilizers**
  Amish gardeners use a variety of organic fertilizers, such as manure, compost, and organic matter, to enrich the soil. Horse, chicken, and cow manure are commonly used in Amish gardens

to provide plants with essential nutrients. These natural fertilizers not only provide the soil with nutrients but also help improve its structure and water retention.

2. Seeds and Plants

Amish gardeners place a strong emphasis on heirloom seeds and non-GMO crops. Heirloom seeds are passed down through generations, and many Amish families have their own collections of seeds that they save each year.

- **Heirloom Seed Catalogs**
  Heirloom seed catalogs are an important resource for Amish gardeners who wish to grow a diverse array of crops. These catalogs offer a variety of vegetable, herb, and flower seeds that are suited to organic gardening practices. Amish gardeners often purchase seeds from trusted sources that specialize in non-GMO, heirloom varieties.
- **Transplants and Seedlings**
  In addition to growing from seed, Amish gardeners also use seedlings and transplants to start their gardens in early spring. These seedlings are often grown in greenhouses or cold frames before being transplanted into the garden when the weather warms. Amish gardeners typically grow their own seedlings but may also purchase transplants from local, trusted farmers.

3. Mulch and Weed Barriers

- **Organic Mulch**
  Amish gardeners use organic mulch made from leaves, straw, grass clippings, or wood chips to cover the soil around plants. Mulching conserves moisture, prevents weeds, and helps regulate soil temperature. Organic mulches also break down over time, adding valuable organic matter to the soil.
- **Weed Barriers**
  Weed barriers, such as landscape fabric or newspaper, are sometimes used by Amish gardeners to suppress weed growth in garden beds. These barriers prevent weeds from competing with crops for nutrients and sunlight. The Amish prefer natural,

biodegradable materials that do not introduce harmful chemicals into the soil.

Where to Buy Amish-Style Gardening Tools and Resources

While many Amish gardening tools are handmade by Amish craftsmen or available from local Amish shops, there are also a variety of online retailers that offer high-quality tools and supplies inspired by Amish traditions. Below is a list of some trusted sources where you can find Amish-style gardening tools, equipment, and supplies:

1. **The Amish Farm and Home Supply Store** – A leading retailer of Amish tools and equipment, specializing in hand tools, gardening supplies, and agricultural products.
2. **Lehmans** – An online store that offers a wide selection of Amish-style gardening tools, including hoes, spades, watering cans, and heirloom seeds.
3. **Gemplers** – A supplier of outdoor equipment and tools with a strong focus on sustainability and quality, offering Amish-style tools and products.
4. **Etsy and Local Craft Fairs** – Many Amish artisans sell their handmade gardening tools and equipment on platforms like Etsy, as well as at local craft fairs and markets in Amish communities.

By purchasing Amish-style tools and resources, you not only invest in quality, durable items but also support traditional craftsmanship and sustainable practices.

Conclusion: Cultivating a Simple, Sustainable Garden

Amish gardening tools and supplies are designed with efficiency, durability, and sustainability in mind. These tools help Amish gardeners maintain a simple, self-sufficient lifestyle that aligns with their values of faith, stewardship, and respect for the earth. Whether you are starting your own garden or looking to update your gardening toolkit, Amish-style tools and practices provide a timeless approach to cultivating a thriving, sustainable garden.

With the right tools, resources, and knowledge, you can create a garden that not only nourishes your body but also reflects the principles of simplicity, sustainability, and harmony with nature—just as Amish gardeners have done for centuries.

Appendix 2: Seasonal Gardening Calendar

A Month-by-Month Guide for Amish-Style Gardening

Gardening, especially in the Amish tradition, follows the natural rhythm of the seasons. Each month offers specific tasks and goals to help ensure a bountiful and healthy garden. From preparing the soil in early spring to harvesting and preserving the bounty in the fall, the Amish gardening calendar is designed to help families make the most of every season. Amish gardeners work in harmony with the land, aligning their gardening practices with the changing weather and natural cycles.

This month-by-month guide outlines key gardening tasks and activities, inspired by traditional Amish methods, that will help you maintain a thriving garden throughout the year. While weather patterns and growing conditions may vary depending on your region, these tasks provide a general framework for organic, sustainable gardening.

January: Preparing for the Year Ahead

- **Review Gardening Plans**: January is the perfect time to reflect on last year's garden and make plans for the coming season. Review the successes and challenges of the past year, and take notes on what worked well and what could be improved.
- **Order Seeds**: Now is the time to order seeds, especially heirloom varieties. Amish gardeners typically order seeds in January or early February to ensure they have them ready for planting in the spring. Focus on selecting seeds that are well-suited to your climate and soil conditions.
- **Organize Tools and Equipment**: Take time to clean and organize your tools and gardening supplies. Check for any tools that need to be repaired or replaced, and ensure that all equipment is in good working order for the upcoming gardening season.
- **Study Gardening Resources**: Winter is a good time to read gardening books, watch educational videos, or attend local workshops on organic gardening. Amish families often gather

together to share knowledge and learn from one another during the winter months.

February: Indoor Preparation and Seed Starting

- **Start Seeds Indoors**: February is a key month for starting seeds indoors, particularly for crops that have a longer growing season, such as tomatoes, peppers, and onions. Amish gardeners often use homemade seed trays, wooden boxes, or biodegradable pots for seed starting. Keep the trays in a warm, sunny spot to encourage germination.
- **Prepare Garden Beds**: If the weather allows, start preparing garden beds by removing weeds, breaking up compacted soil, and adding compost or organic matter. Amish gardeners often focus on creating nutrient-rich, well-aerated soil in the early months of the year.
- **Check Seed Supplies**: While starting seeds indoors, double-check your seed stock and make sure that you have enough seeds for the year ahead. Amish gardeners often save seeds from previous years, ensuring that they have a reliable supply of high-quality, non-GMO seeds.

March: Preparing the Garden for Planting

- **Finish Soil Preparation**: As the last frosts begin to thaw, work on your garden beds by turning the soil, incorporating compost, and setting up any necessary row covers. Amish gardeners use manual tillers, broadforks, and hand tools to prepare the soil without disturbing its natural structure.
- **Plant Cold-Weather Crops**: March is the time to plant cold-hardy crops like peas, spinach, lettuce, kale, and radishes. These crops can withstand light frosts and will begin to grow as temperatures warm up.
- **Set Up Cold Frames**: For early spring planting, cold frames are essential. These simple structures help protect young plants from the lingering chill of early spring. Amish gardeners use

cold frames made from wood and glass or plastic to create a warm microenvironment for delicate seedlings.

April: Planting and Early Care

- **Plant Early Crops**: By April, most areas can start planting additional early crops like carrots, beets, and turnips. These root vegetables thrive in cooler weather and can be direct-seeded into the soil.
- **Thin Seedlings**: If you've started seeds indoors, begin thinning the seedlings as they grow to give them space. This ensures that each plant has enough room to grow strong and healthy.
- **Water and Mulch**: Ensure your garden beds are adequately watered, especially during dry spells. Apply a layer of mulch to retain moisture, suppress weeds, and regulate soil temperature. Amish gardeners often use straw, grass clippings, or leaves as mulch.

May: Full Swing Planting and Weed Control

- **Plant Warm-Weather Crops**: May is the time to plant crops like tomatoes, peppers, squash, cucumbers, and beans, which require warmer soil and air temperatures. Make sure the danger of frost has passed before planting these sensitive crops.
- **Transplant Seedlings**: If you started seeds indoors, transplant them into the garden once the soil is warm enough. Handle the seedlings carefully and provide shade or protection from harsh sun until they adjust to the outdoor environment.
- **Weed and Mulch**: Weeding is crucial in May, as weeds will start to compete with your plants for nutrients and water. Amish gardeners often pull weeds by hand or use simple tools like hoes to keep the garden beds clear. After weeding, apply a fresh layer of mulch to suppress future weed growth.

June: Growing and Maintenance

- **Maintain Watering**: During the warmer months, watering is key. Amish gardeners often use watering cans or drip irrigation to provide consistent moisture to the garden without over-saturating the soil.
- **Prune and Support Plants**: Begin staking tall plants like tomatoes, beans, and peppers. Amish gardeners use simple wooden stakes, twine, or cages to support plants and keep them upright as they grow. Prune any dead or damaged foliage to encourage better airflow and prevent disease.
- **Monitor for Pests**: As the garden grows, pests can become a concern. Amish gardeners typically use organic pest control methods, such as companion planting, neem oil, or insecticidal soap, to manage common pests like aphids, caterpillars, and beetles.

July: Harvesting Early Crops and Summer Maintenance

- **Harvest Early Crops**: By July, many of the early crops, such as lettuce, spinach, peas, and radishes, will be ready for harvest. Amish gardeners harvest these crops regularly to encourage continued production and prevent bolting.
- **Mulch and Water**: The summer heat can stress plants, so continue to mulch to retain moisture and protect the soil. Water your garden consistently, particularly during dry spells.
- **Monitor for Disease**: Keep an eye on your plants for signs of disease, especially as the weather warms. Amish gardeners use organic methods like compost tea or beneficial fungi to prevent and treat fungal diseases like blight and mildew.

August: Full Harvest and Preservation

- **Harvest Main Crops**: August is often the peak of the harvest season. Crops like tomatoes, beans, cucumbers, and squash are typically ready for picking. Amish gardeners begin harvesting

regularly to ensure that they are able to preserve the bounty for the winter months.
- **Preserve the Harvest**: Start canning, freezing, and drying your crops to ensure a supply of food through the winter. Amish gardeners can large batches of tomatoes, beans, corn, and other vegetables, storing them in jars for later use. They also begin drying herbs, fruits, and beans.
- **Continue Weed Management**: Keep weeding and maintaining your garden throughout the summer. Weeds can compete with plants for nutrients and water, so regular weeding ensures that your crops thrive.

September: Fall Planting and Preservation

- **Plant Fall Crops**: In September, begin planting fall crops like cabbage, kale, carrots, and turnips. These crops thrive in cooler temperatures and will be ready for harvest in late fall or early winter.
- **Harvest Late Crops**: Continue harvesting late-season crops, including pumpkins, potatoes, and squash. These crops are typically stored for the winter months or used for canning and preserving.
- **Canning and Freezing**: September is a busy time for preserving food. Amish gardeners focus on canning pickles, tomatoes, and other vegetables, as well as freezing beans, peas, and other late-season produce.

October: Final Harvest and Garden Clean-Up

- **Harvest the Last of the Crops**: As the weather cools, it's time to harvest any remaining crops, such as late tomatoes, squash, and cabbage. Be sure to harvest before the first frost hits, as freezing temperatures can damage produce.
- **Prepare the Garden for Winter**: Begin cleaning up the garden by removing dead plants, composting any organic material, and preparing the soil for the winter months. Amish gardeners often

use this time to add a layer of compost or mulch to the garden beds.
- **Save Seeds**: October is also the time to save seeds from your best crops to plant in the following year. Many Amish gardeners save heirloom seeds from their own gardens, ensuring a steady supply of non-GMO, high-quality seeds for the next planting season.

November: Rest and Reflection

- **Reflect on the Season**: As the gardening season winds down, Amish families take time to reflect on the year's work. This is a time to review what worked well in the garden and what could be improved in the coming season.
- **Prepare Tools for Winter**: Clean, sharpen, and store all your gardening tools for the winter. Proper tool maintenance ensures that they will be ready for the next growing season.
- **Prepare for Winter Gardening**: If you plan to garden in the winter, this is a good time to set up cold frames, greenhouses, or indoor gardening systems to continue growing herbs or winter greens.

December: Winter Rest and Preparation

- **Rest and Recharge**: December is a time for Amish families to rest and spend time indoors. The garden is dormant, and gardeners reflect on their efforts over the year and prepare for the upcoming season.
- **Plan for Next Year**: Use this time to plan your next garden. Review seed catalogs, sketch out your garden layout, and decide on the crops you want to grow in the coming season.

Conclusion: Living with the Seasons

The Amish gardening calendar is a guide for working with the seasons and aligning gardening practices with nature's rhythms. From soil preparation in early spring to preserving the harvest in the fall, the Amish approach to gardening reflects their deep connection to the land and their commitment to sustainability, simplicity, and faith. By following this month-by-month guide, you can create a thriving garden that nourishes your body, mind, and soul year-round.

Appendix 3: Growing Heirloom Varieties

A Comprehensive List of Heirloom Seeds and Plants Favored by the Amish

The Amish have long been dedicated to preserving and cultivating heirloom varieties of plants. Heirloom seeds, passed down from generation to generation, are prized for their adaptability, flavor, and ability to thrive in local climates. The Amish community takes great care in selecting seeds that produce reliable, nutritious crops while maintaining genetic diversity. Heirloom gardening not only connects the Amish to their past but also promotes sustainable gardening practices and food sovereignty.

In this section, we will explore a selection of heirloom varieties commonly grown in Amish gardens. These plants are selected for their hardiness, flavor, and resistance to disease, and many have become staples in Amish kitchens and homesteads. Whether you're an experienced gardener or just starting out, this list will introduce you to some of the best heirloom varieties to grow in your own garden.

1. Heirloom Vegetables: Hardy and Flavorful

Heirloom vegetables are a cornerstone of Amish gardens, offering flavors and textures that are often superior to those of modern hybrid varieties. These varieties are typically open-pollinated, meaning they will produce seeds that are true to type and can be saved year after year.

Tomatoes: A Favorite Amish Crop

Tomatoes are a staple in the Amish garden, prized for their rich flavor and versatility in cooking. Many Amish gardeners grow heirloom tomato varieties, which are known for their thick skins, full flavor, and ability to be used for everything from fresh eating to canning.

- **Brandywine**: This heirloom variety is one of the most popular among Amish gardeners. Known for its large, pinkish-red fruit,

Brandywine tomatoes are rich and meaty, making them perfect for sandwiches, sauces, and canning.
- **Cherokee Purple**: A favorite for its deep, smoky flavor, Cherokee Purple tomatoes have a distinctive dark hue and are often used in fresh salsas or as a topping for sandwiches.
- **Mortgage Lifter**: Known for its large fruit and excellent flavor, Mortgage Lifter tomatoes are ideal for canning and making sauces. These heirloom tomatoes have been passed down through generations and are highly valued by the Amish.

Peppers: Sweet and Spicy Varieties

Peppers are another essential crop in Amish gardens. Whether sweet or hot, peppers add flavor and variety to Amish meals and are often preserved through canning or drying.

- **Sweet Banana Pepper**: A popular choice among Amish gardeners, these mild peppers are perfect for pickling. Their long, slender shape and bright yellow color make them a beautiful addition to any garden.
- **Cayenne**: For those who enjoy a bit of heat, the Cayenne pepper is a must. Amish gardeners often grow this spicy variety to use in sauces, powders, and spice blends. It's also great for drying and storing for later use.
- **Jimmy Nardello**: A sweet, thin-walled pepper that is perfect for roasting, frying, or making into pepper jelly. This heirloom variety is favored for its unique flavor and thin skin.

Beans: Versatile and Nutritious

Beans are an essential protein source in the Amish diet, and heirloom varieties are often favored for their rich flavor and hearty texture. Beans are typically grown in large quantities, harvested, and then dried for long-term storage.

- **Jacob's Cattle Bean**: A traditional Amish variety known for its speckled red and white beans. Jacob's Cattle beans are often used in soups, stews, and baked beans, and they are also a staple in Amish canning.

- **Red Kidney Bean**: Known for its rich, hearty flavor, the Red Kidney Bean is often grown by Amish gardeners for use in winter soups and chili. These beans are great for drying and storing.
- **Blue Lake Bean**: This classic heirloom variety produces tender green beans that are perfect for fresh eating or canning. The Blue Lake bean is a staple in Amish gardens for its disease resistance and productivity.

Cabbage and Brassicas: Crucial for Winter Preservation

Brassicas, including cabbage, kale, and broccoli, are important in Amish gardens due to their ability to survive cooler temperatures and provide hearty meals during the winter months. These crops are often stored in root cellars and used for preserving.

- **Savoy Cabbage**: Known for its crinkly, tender leaves, Savoy cabbage is a favorite for Amish gardeners. It is great for making coleslaw, sauerkraut, and other preserved dishes.
- **Breen Kale**: A hardy, flavorful variety of kale, Breen kale is often grown for its ability to survive in colder temperatures and provide fresh greens well into the fall.
- **De Cicco Broccoli**: An early variety of broccoli that matures quickly and produces compact heads. Amish gardeners favor this heirloom for its tenderness and high yield.

2. Heirloom Fruits: Sweet, Juicy, and Rich in Flavor

Heirloom fruits are often cultivated in Amish orchards and backyard gardens. These fruits are known for their deep flavors and rich textures, and they are often used for making preserves, pies, and jams.

Apples: The Amish Orchard Staple

Apples are one of the most popular fruits grown in Amish gardens, and heirloom apple varieties are prized for their crisp texture and complex flavors.

- **Winesap**: A classic heirloom apple variety, Winesap apples are known for their tart, spicy flavor, making them perfect for baking and making cider. These apples are a staple in Amish orchards.
- **Gravenstein**: This early-season apple is prized for its sweet, tangy flavor. Amish gardeners grow Gravensteins for fresh eating, pies, and applesauce. The apples are also excellent for juicing and making cider.
- **Jonathan**: A popular apple variety that produces small, red apples with a sharp, tangy taste. Jonathan apples are great for fresh eating, baking, and making applesauce.

Peaches: Juicy and Sweet

Peaches thrive in Amish gardens, especially in areas with a warm climate. Heirloom peach varieties are particularly sought after for their sweetness and juiciness.

- **Elberta**: A classic heirloom peach variety, Elberta peaches are large, juicy, and sweet. These peaches are perfect for canning, pies, or simply enjoying fresh off the tree.
- **Belle of Georgia**: A freestone peach that is known for its sweet, fragrant flavor. Amish gardeners often grow Belle of Georgia for use in preserves and jams.
- **Red Haven**: One of the earliest varieties of peaches to ripen, Red Haven peaches are prized for their smooth texture and balanced sweetness.

Strawberries: Sweet and Tangy

Strawberries are another favorite fruit in Amish gardens. The Amish often grow strawberries in raised beds or along fences to maximize their production and minimize the risk of rot.

- **June-bearing**: This heirloom variety produces large, sweet strawberries early in the season. June-bearing strawberries are ideal for preserving and are often used to make strawberry jam, jelly, or pies.
- **Quinault**: A perpetual-bearing variety, Quinault strawberries produce fruit throughout the growing season. These

strawberries are smaller but very flavorful, perfect for fresh eating.

3. Heirloom Herbs: Flavorful and Medicinal

Herbs are a key component of the Amish garden, providing flavor for cooking, as well as medicinal benefits. Many heirloom herbs are passed down through generations for their culinary and healing properties.

Basil: A Garden Favorite

Basil is one of the most popular herbs in Amish gardens, known for its aromatic leaves that add flavor to a variety of dishes.

- **Genovese Basil**: This traditional Italian basil variety is favored for its large, aromatic leaves. Amish gardeners grow Genovese basil for use in pesto, sauces, and fresh salads.
- **Thai Basil**: With its spicy, licorice-like flavor, Thai basil is used in Asian-inspired dishes and is highly prized for its unique flavor. It grows well in Amish gardens and is often dried or used fresh.

Mint: Versatile and Refreshing

Mint is another staple in Amish gardens, known for its refreshing taste and variety of uses. Amish gardeners grow both culinary and medicinal varieties of mint.

- **Peppermint**: This popular mint variety is commonly used to make teas, sauces, and jellies. It also has medicinal uses, particularly for soothing digestive issues.
- **Spearmint**: Another commonly grown mint, spearmint has a milder flavor and is often used in beverages, salads, and desserts.

Thyme: A Flavorful Herb

Thyme is a versatile herb that thrives in Amish gardens. It is prized for its robust flavor and is used in a variety of savory dishes.

- **English Thyme**: Known for its aromatic leaves, English thyme is used to flavor soups, stews, meats, and vegetables. It is hardy and easy to grow, making it a staple herb in Amish gardens.
- **Lemon Thyme**: This variety has a subtle lemon fragrance, making it ideal for pairing with chicken, fish, and Mediterranean dishes.

4. Growing Heirloom Varieties: Key Considerations

When growing heirloom varieties, there are a few important factors to consider to ensure the best results:

- **Soil Preparation**: Heirloom varieties thrive in well-prepared soil that is rich in organic matter. Amish gardeners focus on soil health by using compost, manure, and crop rotation to maintain fertility.
- **Seed Saving**: One of the key benefits of growing heirloom plants is the ability to save seeds for future seasons. Amish gardeners often save the seeds from their best plants to ensure a continuous supply of heirloom varieties. To save seeds, choose healthy, disease-free plants, and allow them to fully ripen before harvesting the seeds.
- **Climate and Growing Conditions**: Each heirloom variety has specific growing conditions. Amish gardeners select varieties that are suited to their local climate and growing zone, ensuring that the plants will thrive and produce a bountiful harvest.

Conclusion: A Legacy of Flavor and Sustainability

Heirloom gardening is a tradition that not only connects the Amish to their past but also provides a sustainable, diverse, and flavorful future.

By cultivating these time-honored varieties, Amish gardeners preserve the rich history of food production and ensure that the flavors and benefits of these crops continue to nourish their families for generations to come.

Whether you are growing tomatoes, herbs, or fruit trees, choosing heirloom varieties is a step toward fostering biodiversity, sustainability, and a deep connection to the land. By incorporating these heirloom seeds and plants into your own garden, you can embrace the values of simplicity, sustainability, and self-sufficiency that define Amish gardening.

Appendix 4: Harvesting and Preservation Charts

A Detailed Guide to Harvesting Times and Methods

In Amish gardening, harvesting and preserving the crops are just as important as planting them. The Amish focus on maintaining a steady food supply throughout the year by knowing exactly when to harvest their crops at the peak of ripeness and how to preserve them for winter use. This detailed guide will help you understand when to harvest various vegetables, fruits, and herbs and how to preserve them using traditional methods like canning, freezing, and drying. Proper timing and techniques ensure that your food is both flavorful and safe for consumption.

Whether you're working with a variety of crops or focusing on a few key harvests, following the right harvesting and preservation methods can make a world of difference in both the quality and shelf-life of your food. Here, we've compiled essential charts for harvesting and preserving the bounty from your garden.

Harvesting and Preservation Chart for Vegetables

Vegetable	Harvesting Time	Preservation Method	Method Details
Tomatoes	When fully colored, firm, and ripe (varies by variety)	Canning, Freezing, Drying	**Canning**: Blanch, peel, and can in jars with water or sauce. **Freezing**: Freeze after blanching or raw. **Drying**: Slice and dry using a dehydrator or in the sun.
Cucumbers	Harvest when firm and before seeds become large	Pickling, Canning, Freezing	**Pickling**: Cut into spears or slices, can with vinegar, water, and spices. **Freezing**: Blanch and freeze for later use in soups.

Vegetable	Harvesting Time	Preservation Method	Method Details
Carrots	When roots are large, firm, and bright in color	Freezing, Root Cellar Storage	**Freezing**: Peel, cut, blanch, and freeze. **Root Cellar**: Store in moist sand or soil in a cool, dark place.
Beans (Snap)	When pods are firm, crisp, and bright (harvest early for snap beans)	Freezing, Canning	**Freezing**: Blanch beans briefly, then freeze. **Canning**: Pack in jars with water and pressure cook.
Peas	When pods are swollen, but before they dry out	Freezing, Canning	**Freezing**: Blanch peas and freeze. **Canning**: Can in jars with water.
Potatoes	After vines die back (for storage), when skins are firm	Root Cellar Storage, Freezing	**Root Cellar**: Cure for a few days, then store in a cool, dry place. **Freezing**: Peel, blanch, and freeze.
Squash (Winter)	Harvest when skin is hard, color is rich, and stem is dry	Canning, Freezing, Root Cellar Storage	**Canning**: Steam or bake, then can with water or syrup. **Freezing**: Cook, puree, and freeze. **Root Cellar**: Store whole in a cool, dark place.
Kale	After leaves are fully mature but tender, harvest outer leaves first	Freezing, Drying, Eating Fresh	**Freezing**: Blanch, then freeze. **Drying**: Dehydrate leaves.
Lettuce (Leaf)	When leaves are large and vibrant	Drying, Freezing, Fresh	**Freezing**: Freeze in airtight bags. **Fresh**: Use immediately, or keep in the fridge.

Vegetable	Harvesting Time	Preservation Method	Method Details
Spinach	When leaves are large and tender	Freezing, Drying, Canning	**Freezing**: Blanch and freeze. **Drying**: Air dry or use a dehydrator.

Harvesting and Preservation Chart for Fruits

Fruit	Harvesting Time	Preservation Method	Method Details
Apples	When fruits are fully colored and slightly soft to the touch	Canning, Freezing, Drying	**Canning**: Peel and can in syrup or juice. **Freezing**: Slice and freeze after blanching. **Drying**: Slice and dry.
Peaches	When fully ripe, soft to the touch, and fragrant	Canning, Freezing	**Canning**: Peel, slice, and can in syrup or juice. **Freezing**: Peel, slice, and freeze in airtight bags.
Pears	When fruits yield slightly to gentle pressure	Canning, Freezing	**Canning**: Peel, core, and can in syrup. **Freezing**: Peel, slice, and freeze in sugar syrup.
Cherries	When fully ripe and sweet	Canning, Freezing	**Canning**: Pit and can with syrup. **Freezing**: Pit and freeze in airtight bags.
Strawberries	When bright red, firm, and juicy	Freezing, Jam, Canning	**Freezing**: Freeze after washing and hulling. **Jam**: Make strawberry jam with sugar and pectin.
Raspberries	When fully ripe and juicy	Freezing, Jam	**Freezing**: Freeze whole berries. **Jam**:

Fruit	Harvesting Time	Preservation Method	Method Details
Blackberries	When fully ripe and sweet	Freezing, Jam	Make raspberry jam with sugar and pectin. **Freezing**: Freeze whole berries. **Jam**: Make blackberry jam.
Grapes	When fully ripe and berries are plump and juicy	Jelly, Canning, Freezing	**Canning**: Can grape juice or jelly. **Freezing**: Freeze grapes for snacks or smoothies.
Plums	When fully ripe, soft, and fragrant	Canning, Freezing	**Canning**: Can whole or as jam. **Freezing**: Pit, slice, and freeze.

Harvesting and Preservation Chart for Herbs

Herb	Harvesting Time	Preservation Method	Method Details
Basil	Before flowering, when leaves are full and aromatic	Drying, Freezing, Pesto	**Drying**: Dry by hanging in bundles or using a dehydrator. **Freezing**: Freeze in ice cube trays with olive oil. **Pesto**: Make pesto and freeze in small portions.
Oregano	When leaves are fully mature but still tender	Drying, Freezing	**Drying**: Dry by hanging upside down or in a dehydrator. **Freezing**: Freeze in airtight bags.
Thyme	Just before flowering when leaves are aromatic	Drying, Freezing	**Drying**: Hang in bunches or use a dehydrator. **Freezing**: Freeze in airtight bags or ice cube trays.
Rosemary	Before flowering, when	Drying, Freezing	**Drying**: Hang or dry in a dehydrator. **Freezing**:

Herb	Harvesting Time	Preservation Method	Method Details
	leaves are aromatic and full		Freeze in airtight bags or ice cube trays.
Mint	When leaves are vibrant and fragrant, before flowering	Drying, Freezing	**Drying**: Hang upside down or use a dehydrator. **Freezing**: Freeze mint leaves in ice cube trays.
Sage	After the first frost but before snow, when leaves are aromatic	Drying, Freezing	**Drying**: Hang or use a dehydrator. **Freezing**: Freeze in airtight bags.

General Tips for Harvesting and Preserving

- **Timing is Key**: The timing of your harvest is essential for the best flavor and quality of preserved food. Harvest vegetables in the morning, after the dew has evaporated, and fruits when they are fully ripe but firm.
- **Cleanliness**: Always wash produce thoroughly before preserving, but be gentle to avoid bruising. For herbs, remove dirt and moisture before drying.
- **Use Proper Containers**: For canning, always use sterilized jars and new lids. For freezing, ensure airtight containers or bags are used to prevent freezer burn.
- **Proper Canning Techniques**: Follow specific canning instructions for each fruit or vegetable to ensure safe preservation. The Amish traditionally rely on water-bath and pressure canning to preserve food for long-term storage.
- **Storage**: For dried herbs and fruits, store them in cool, dark, and dry places. Root cellars are ideal for storing root vegetables like potatoes, carrots, and turnips through the winter.

Conclusion: Building Your Pantry with the Harvest

The act of harvesting and preserving your garden's bounty is deeply satisfying and ties you to the earth and its natural rhythms. By following the harvesting and preservation methods outlined in these charts, you can enjoy the fruits of your labor throughout the year, just as the Amish have done for generations. Whether you're enjoying fresh tomatoes in the summer, winter squash in the fall, or herb-infused dishes in the winter months, preserving the harvest is a way of ensuring that your efforts provide nourishment for your family for months to come.

By carefully timing your harvests, using organic methods, and preserving food through traditional techniques, you can create a sustainable, healthy food system that not only nourishes your body but also brings you closer to the rhythms of nature.

Appendix 5: Amish Gardening Techniques and Processes

A Simple and Sustainable Approach

Gardening is both an art and a science. Amish gardeners have refined their techniques over generations to grow healthy, vibrant crops using simple, sustainable methods. These practices focus on working with nature rather than against it. Below is a breakdown of essential gardening techniques and processes, explained in a straightforward and easy-to-understand way.

1. Soil Preparation: The Foundation for Healthy Plants

Healthy soil is the cornerstone of a thriving garden. Amish gardeners put a lot of effort into preparing the soil, as it provides the nutrients and structure plants need to grow strong.

Key Processes:

- **Clearing the Garden Bed**: Before planting, Amish gardeners clear the garden of weeds, dead plants, and debris. This ensures that no unwanted plants compete for space or nutrients with the crops.
- **Tilling or Loosening the Soil**: Amish gardeners often use simple tools like hoes, spades, or broadforks to break up compacted soil. This allows air and water to reach the roots, which helps plants grow better. Instead of heavy tilling, Amish gardeners use gentle methods to maintain soil structure.
- **Adding Organic Matter**: To improve soil fertility and structure, Amish gardeners add organic materials like compost, aged manure, or grass clippings. Organic matter helps retain moisture, supports healthy root systems, and provides essential nutrients for plants.

Why It Matters:

Healthy, well-prepared soil improves plant growth, reduces the need for fertilizers, and helps retain moisture during dry spells. Amish gardening emphasizes soil health through natural methods, ensuring sustainable farming year after year.

2. Crop Rotation: Keep the Soil Healthy and Productive

Crop rotation is a gardening technique where different crops are planted in different spots each season. This prevents the soil from becoming depleted of specific nutrients and helps break pest and disease cycles.

Key Processes:

- **Plan Your Crop Rotation**: Amish gardeners rotate crops to balance the nutrients in the soil. For example, legumes (like beans) fix nitrogen in the soil, while leafy greens (like lettuce) need lots of nitrogen. After growing nitrogen-hungry crops like lettuce, Amish gardeners will plant legumes to restore soil nutrients.
- **Group Crops by Family**: Crops in the same plant family (e.g., tomatoes, peppers, and eggplant are all part of the nightshade family) tend to require similar nutrients and are more likely to share pests and diseases. Amish gardeners group different plant families in different garden areas each season to minimize these risks.

Why It Matters:

Crop rotation helps maintain soil fertility, reduces pest problems, and ensures that the garden remains productive for years without relying on synthetic fertilizers.

3. Companion Planting: Growing Plants That Help Each Other

Companion planting involves planting certain crops together that benefit one another. This method is natural, organic, and an essential part of Amish gardening practices. Some plants can repel pests, attract beneficial insects, or improve soil health when planted together.

Key Processes:

- **Choose Beneficial Plant Combinations**: For example, planting marigolds with tomatoes helps repel aphids and other pests. Planting basil with peppers can enhance their flavor and protect against insects.
- **Use Plants to Enhance Growth**: Some plants, like beans, are nitrogen-fixers, meaning they add nitrogen to the soil, which is beneficial for crops like corn or tomatoes. Amish gardeners often plant beans next to these crops to naturally boost soil health.

Why It Matters:

Companion planting reduces the need for pesticides and helps plants grow stronger and healthier by fostering natural relationships between different species. Amish gardening values working with nature's cycles.

4. Mulching: Protecting the Soil and Plants

Mulching is the process of covering the soil around plants with organic or inorganic materials. It helps retain moisture, suppresses weeds, and regulates soil temperature.

Key Processes:

- **Choose Your Mulch**: Common organic mulches include straw, grass clippings, leaves, and wood chips. These materials break down over time, adding nutrients to the soil.
- **Apply Mulch Around Plants**: Spread a 2- to 4-inch layer of mulch around the base of plants, but make sure not to pile it directly against plant stems, as this can cause rot.

Why It Matters:

Mulch helps conserve water, suppress weeds, and prevent the soil from drying out in hot weather. It's a simple, effective way to improve plant health without using synthetic chemicals.

5. Hand Weeding: Keeping the Garden Free of Unwanted Plants

Weeds compete with your crops for nutrients, water, and sunlight. Amish gardeners rely on hand weeding as their primary method for keeping gardens weed-free.

Key Processes:

- **Weeding by Hand**: Amish gardeners often use simple tools like hoes, hand forks, or even their hands to pull weeds from garden beds. It's best to remove weeds early in the growing season, before they flower and set seed.
- **Mulch to Prevent Weeds**: Once the weeds are removed, a fresh layer of mulch is often applied to suppress new weed growth.

Why It Matters:

Weeds can choke out garden crops, so regular weeding is essential for maintaining healthy plants. Hand weeding is effective because it avoids the use of harmful chemicals and preserves the soil's natural health.

6. Watering: Ensuring Consistent Moisture for Healthy Growth

Proper watering is critical for plant health. Amish gardeners rely on several methods to ensure their plants get the right amount of moisture.

Key Processes:

- **Water Early in the Day**: To avoid evaporation, Amish gardeners often water in the morning, giving plants enough time to absorb water before the heat of the day.
- **Use Watering Cans or Drip Irrigation**: While modern sprinklers are avoided, Amish gardeners often use simple watering cans or drip irrigation systems, which provide consistent and targeted moisture to plant roots.

Why It Matters:

Watering at the right time and in the right way ensures plants get the moisture they need without wasting water or encouraging disease. Amish gardeners prioritize efficient, sustainable watering methods that reduce the impact on the environment.

7. Harvesting: Knowing When and How to Collect Your Crops

Harvesting at the right time is key to preserving the best flavor and nutritional value of crops. Amish gardeners are careful to harvest crops at their peak of ripeness.

Key Processes:

- **Harvest at Peak Ripeness**: For vegetables like tomatoes, peppers, and beans, harvest when they are fully ripe but not overripe. For root crops like carrots and potatoes, harvest when the plants' tops begin to die back or when the roots have reached a good size.
- **Handle Plants Gently**: Amish gardeners are careful when harvesting to avoid bruising or damaging the produce. They often use baskets or wooden crates to carry their harvests back to the house.

Why It Matters:

Properly timed harvests ensure the best quality crops and allow for efficient storage or preservation. Harvesting too early or too late can reduce the flavor and nutritional value of your produce.

8. Preservation Methods: Storing Your Harvest for Year-Round Enjoyment

Once the crops are harvested, Amish gardeners use a variety of preservation methods to store food for the winter months. These methods include canning, freezing, drying, and root cellaring.

Key Processes:

- **Canning**: This involves sealing food in jars and processing them with heat to kill bacteria and preserve the food for long-term storage. Commonly canned items include tomatoes, beans, and fruits.
- **Freezing**: For vegetables and fruits like peas, beans, and strawberries, freezing is a great option. Blanch the produce briefly, then freeze it in airtight bags to preserve flavor and texture.
- **Drying**: Herbs, tomatoes, and fruits like apples and peaches can be dried in a dehydrator or under the sun to preserve them for months. Dried foods are stored in airtight containers and used in cooking throughout the year.
- **Root Cellaring**: Root vegetables like potatoes, carrots, and turnips are stored in cool, dark, humid conditions in a root cellar, which prevents spoilage and keeps them fresh for months.

Why It Matters:

Preserving your garden's bounty ensures that you have access to fresh, nutritious food all year long. Amish gardeners rely on these preservation methods to store food without relying on refrigeration or modern conveniences.

9. Saving Seeds: Replenishing Your Stock for the Next Season

Saving seeds is a critical part of Amish gardening. It allows gardeners to preserve heirloom varieties and maintain self-sufficiency.

Key Processes:

- **Select the Best Plants**: Amish gardeners select the healthiest, most productive plants to save seeds from. This ensures that the seeds will produce strong, reliable crops the following year.
- **Proper Seed Storage**: Seeds are dried thoroughly and stored in cool, dry conditions. Amish gardeners often use paper envelopes, glass jars, or small wooden boxes to store seeds until planting time.

Why It Matters:

Saving seeds allows Amish gardeners to grow the same high-quality, non-GMO crops year after year without needing to purchase new seeds. It also helps preserve the genetic diversity of heirloom varieties.

Conclusion: Simple Techniques for a Thriving Garden

The Amish approach to gardening revolves around simplicity, sustainability, and a deep connection to the land. By following these basic techniques, Amish gardeners grow healthy, productive crops without the need for modern technology or synthetic chemicals. Whether you're planting your first garden or are an experienced gardener, these methods will help you create a thriving, self-sufficient garden that produces bountiful harvests year after year.

By embracing these Amish-inspired techniques, you can cultivate a garden that nurtures not only your body but also your connection to nature and the rhythms of the seasons.

Glossary

This glossary provides definitions of essential terms related to Amish gardening, preservation methods, and the tools and practices commonly used in Amish homesteads. These terms will help clarify the methods, tools, and practices used by Amish gardeners to grow, harvest, and preserve their crops throughout the year.

A

- **Aeration**: The process of introducing air into the soil to improve root growth and nutrient absorption. Amish gardeners often use tools like broadforks or hand cultivators to loosen the soil, improving aeration and helping plants grow more efficiently.
- **Amish Heirloom Seeds**: Open-pollinated seeds that have been passed down through generations. These seeds are cherished for their ability to produce consistent and flavorful crops, and they are typically non-GMO. Amish gardeners preserve heirloom seeds each year to maintain biodiversity and promote self-sufficiency.

B

- **Biodiversity**: The variety of plant and animal life in a particular habitat. In Amish gardening, biodiversity is encouraged through practices like companion planting and crop rotation, which help protect the garden from pests and diseases while improving soil health.
- **Broadfork**: A garden tool used for aerating and loosening soil without turning it over. This method preserves soil structure and improves root health, a technique commonly used in Amish gardens to prepare beds for planting.

C

- **Cold Frame**: A simple structure, often made of wood and glass or plastic, used to protect plants from the cold by trapping solar heat. Amish gardeners use cold frames to extend the growing season for early or late crops and to harden off seedlings before transplanting them outdoors.
- **Companion Planting**: A gardening technique in which certain plants are grown together to promote healthy growth and deter pests. For example, planting marigolds with tomatoes helps repel aphids. Amish gardeners use companion planting extensively as part of their organic practices.
- **Canning**: The process of preserving food by placing it in jars and heating it to kill bacteria, yeast, and molds. Canning allows Amish families to store fruits, vegetables, and meats for long-term use, typically using water-bath or pressure canning methods.

D

- **Dehydrating**: The process of drying food to remove moisture, preventing the growth of bacteria and mold. Amish gardeners often dehydrate herbs, fruits, and vegetables for storage and long-term preservation. The dried foods are stored in airtight containers to maintain freshness.
- **Direct Seeding**: Planting seeds directly into the garden soil rather than starting them indoors. Amish gardeners often direct seed crops like carrots, beans, and peas, which grow well when planted directly in the ground.

F

- **Fermentation**: A method of preserving food through the action of beneficial bacteria. It's commonly used for foods like sauerkraut, pickles, and kimchi. Amish gardeners ferment

cabbage, cucumbers, and other vegetables to create long-lasting and nutritious foods.
- **Frost Date**: The expected date of the first and last frost in a given growing season. Amish gardeners use frost dates to determine the best time to plant and harvest crops. They often use this information to protect plants from early or late frosts.

G

- **Greenhouse**: A structure made of glass or plastic designed to trap sunlight and create a controlled environment for growing plants. Amish gardeners may use greenhouses, often powered by passive solar energy, to grow plants during the colder months or to start seedlings before the outdoor growing season.
- **Grafting**: A method of propagating plants by joining two plants together so that they grow as one. Grafting is often used with fruit trees, and Amish gardeners may graft new varieties onto older, hardier rootstock to improve growth or fruit yield.

H

- **Heirloom Varieties**: Plants that are open-pollinated, passed down through generations, and bred for specific traits. Amish gardeners prioritize heirloom varieties because they are adaptable to the local environment and provide superior flavor and nutrition compared to hybrids.
- **Hotbed**: A gardening structure that uses natural heat to warm the soil, typically created by placing manure underneath the soil surface. Amish gardeners use hotbeds to start early crops in the spring, using heat from the decomposing manure to raise the temperature in the garden.

I

- **Inoculant**: A substance containing beneficial microorganisms added to soil or compost to encourage plant growth. Amish gardeners use natural inoculants to improve soil health, particularly when planting legumes like beans, which benefit from nitrogen-fixing bacteria.
- **Indoor Seed Starting**: The practice of starting seeds indoors before transplanting them into the garden. This method is often used for tender crops like tomatoes and peppers, and Amish gardeners use simple setups such as wooden trays or homemade seed starters to grow seedlings in the winter months.

J

- **Jarring**: The act of preserving fruits and vegetables by placing them in sterilized glass jars and sealing them for storage. This is commonly used in Amish canning practices, where fruits like peaches and tomatoes are placed in jars and sealed to preserve them for the long term.
- **Jelly Making**: The process of cooking fruit juice with sugar and pectin to create jelly. Amish gardeners often make jellies from berries, apples, or grapes, preserving them in jars for long-term storage and future use.

L

- **Layering**: A method of propagating plants by bending a branch to the ground and allowing it to take root while still attached to the parent plant. This technique is used by Amish gardeners for certain shrubs and plants, including berries and grapes, to create new plants.
- **Leaf Mold**: A natural compost made from decomposed leaves. Amish gardeners often collect fallen leaves in the fall, allowing them to break down over time to create leaf mold, which is then used to improve soil texture and fertility.

M

- **Mulching**: The practice of covering the soil with organic or inorganic materials, such as straw, leaves, or grass clippings, to retain moisture, suppress weeds, and regulate soil temperature. Amish gardeners often mulch their garden beds to improve soil health and reduce the need for frequent watering.
- **Manure**: Animal waste used as a natural fertilizer in Amish gardens. Horse, cow, and chicken manure are commonly used to enrich the soil. Amish gardeners typically compost manure to make it safer and more beneficial for plant growth.

P

- **Preserving**: The act of preparing food to be stored for future use, including canning, freezing, drying, and pickling. Amish gardeners preserve their harvest through these methods to ensure that they have a steady food supply throughout the year.
- **Pickling**: The process of preserving vegetables or fruits in brine or vinegar. Commonly used for cucumbers, onions, and beets, pickling is a key method of food preservation in Amish households, often enhanced with garlic, dill, and other spices.

R

- **Root Cellar**: A cool, dark, and humid space used for storing root vegetables like potatoes, carrots, and beets. Amish gardeners use root cellars to keep produce fresh through the winter months, allowing them to harvest crops in the fall and store them for long-term use.
- **Rotation**: The practice of changing the location of crops in a garden each year to prevent soil depletion and reduce the risk of pests and diseases. Amish gardeners rotate crops like beans, corn, and squash, which helps maintain soil fertility.

S

- **Seed Saving**: The practice of collecting and storing seeds from plants to be used for future planting. Amish gardeners often save heirloom seeds from their best crops, ensuring that they have a reliable, high-quality supply for the following year.
- **Seedling**: A young plant grown from a seed, typically started indoors or in a controlled environment before being transplanted into the garden. Amish gardeners often start their seedlings early in the season to ensure a strong start to the growing year.

T

- **Trellis**: A structure used to support climbing plants such as peas, beans, and cucumbers. Amish gardeners often use wooden or metal trellises to keep plants off the ground, promoting better air circulation and reducing the risk of disease.
- **Transplanting**: The process of moving a seedling from one location, typically indoors or in a nursery, to its permanent outdoor garden spot. Amish gardeners often transplant crops like tomatoes and peppers once the soil and weather conditions are favorable.

W

- **Watering Can**: A container with a spout and handle used to water plants by hand. Amish gardeners often use simple, durable watering cans made of metal or plastic for consistent and gentle watering of garden beds.
- **Weeding**: The practice of removing unwanted plants that compete with crops for space, nutrients, and water. Amish gardeners often weed their garden beds by hand or with simple tools like hoes or hand rakes to ensure that their crops thrive.

Z

- **Zoning (Hardiness Zone)**: A classification that defines the average minimum temperature in a region. Amish gardeners use hardiness zone maps to determine which plants will thrive in their specific climate, ensuring that they choose appropriate crops for their growing conditions.

Conclusion: Connecting Knowledge with Practice

This glossary provides definitions of key terms that are integral to Amish gardening and preservation. Understanding these terms will help you navigate the practices, tools, and techniques used by Amish gardeners to create healthy, sustainable, and productive gardens. The Amish approach to gardening emphasizes a connection to the land, patience, and resourcefulness, and by learning these terms and methods, you can begin to implement similar practices in your own garden to ensure a bountiful harvest.

References

This list provides a collection of books, articles, and resources for further reading about Amish gardening practices, culture, sustainability, and the historical evolution of Amish farming. It includes works from Amish experts, communities focused on gardening and self-sufficiency, and historical accounts that explore how Amish farming has evolved over the centuries.

Books on Amish Culture and Sustainability

1. **"The Amish: A Human History" by John A. Hostetler**
   - **Overview**: This book provides an in-depth exploration of Amish culture, history, and lifestyle. John A. Hostetler, a well-known sociologist and expert on Amish life, discusses the Amish commitment to simplicity, self-sufficiency, and their relationship with the land.
   - **Relevance**: Essential for understanding the cultural values that influence Amish farming practices and their emphasis on sustainability.
2. **"The Amish Gardener" by Howard W. Lapp**
   - **Overview**: Lapp's book covers the art of Amish gardening, blending personal anecdotes with practical advice. It delves into the importance of heirloom varieties, organic practices, and maintaining gardens in harmony with nature.
   - **Relevance**: Provides insights into Amish gardening practices, with a focus on self-sufficiency and sustainable gardening methods.
3. **"Living More with Less" by Doris Janzen Longacre**
   - **Overview**: A classic Amish-inspired guide to simple living, this book explores the Amish approach to sustainability, self-reliance, and resourcefulness, touching on gardening, preserving food, and managing household resources.

- **Relevance**: A helpful resource for those interested in adopting Amish principles of simplicity and sustainability in their own lives.
4. **"The Amish: Their Traditions, Beliefs, and Culture" by Donald B. Kraybill**
    - **Overview**: Donald Kraybill is a leading expert on Amish communities. This comprehensive book explains Amish traditions, including farming, food production, and sustainable living, providing a detailed view of Amish culture and how their agricultural practices have shaped their way of life.
    - **Relevance**: Key for understanding the social and cultural framework within which Amish gardening and farming practices have evolved.
5. **"Homemade: A Story of Amish Farm Life" by David Kline**
    - **Overview**: Kline, a former Amish farmer, shares his personal experiences with Amish farming and self-sufficiency. He discusses the integration of faith and farming, as well as the methods and tools used in Amish gardens.
    - **Relevance**: Provides valuable insights into Amish farm life and gardening techniques, particularly focusing on the Amish commitment to self-sufficiency.

Books on Amish Gardening and Sustainable Farming

1. **"Seed to Seed: Seed Saving and Growing Techniques for Vegetable Gardeners" by Suzanne Ashworth**
    - **Overview**: While not exclusively focused on Amish gardening, this book is essential for anyone interested in seed-saving, a practice central to Amish farming. It covers over 160 vegetable species, explaining the best methods for saving and storing seeds.
    - **Relevance**: Heirloom seed-saving is a key aspect of Amish farming, and this book provides guidance that aligns with Amish practices of self-sufficiency and sustainability.

2. **"The Complete Guide to Organic Gardening: A Practical Approach to Growing a Healthy, High-Yielding Garden" by The Organic Gardening Institute**
     - **Overview**: This book discusses organic gardening methods that are key to Amish farming practices, including crop rotation, composting, and natural pest control.
     - **Relevance**: The principles of organic gardening are integral to Amish methods, which are focused on sustainability and environmental stewardship.
3. **"The Amish Garden: A Manual of Practical Tips for Growing Fruits, Vegetables, and Herbs" by Martha Crissman**
     - **Overview**: This book provides detailed tips on growing and maintaining an Amish-style garden, emphasizing low-tech, sustainable approaches to food production. It includes advice on companion planting, using heirloom varieties, and preserving crops.
     - **Relevance**: A practical guide for those wishing to replicate Amish gardening methods, from seed starting to harvesting and preserving.
4. **"Growing with the Seasons: Amish Gardening Wisdom for Every Season" by Rachel Heisey**
     - **Overview**: A comprehensive guide that covers Amish gardening practices through each season. It focuses on planting schedules, soil health, crop rotation, and preserving the harvest.
     - **Relevance**: This book is perfect for understanding how Amish gardeners plan and manage their gardens year-round, ensuring food security and sustainability.

Notable Amish Experts and Communities Focused on Gardening and Sustainability

1. **The Amish Acres Homestead and Gardens** (Indiana, USA)
     - **Overview**: Amish Acres is a historical Amish community in Indiana known for its sustainable farming practices, traditional architecture, and organic

gardening. They are committed to preserving traditional farming methods and educating the public on Amish practices of gardening, agriculture, and sustainability.
    - **Relevance**: A prime example of an Amish community dedicated to preserving their farming heritage and teaching others about sustainable gardening practices.
2. **Amish Family Farm, Inc.** (Ohio, USA)
    - **Overview**: This family-owned farm in Ohio grows organic vegetables and uses traditional Amish farming methods to maintain sustainability. They are known for their heirloom seed collections and their focus on soil health and preservation.
    - **Relevance**: A real-world example of modern Amish farming, with a strong emphasis on organic gardening and preserving heirloom varieties.
3. **Old Order Amish Communities (Various Locations)**
    - **Overview**: Old Order Amish communities, especially those in Pennsylvania, Ohio, and Indiana, are known for their traditional farming methods. They grow and preserve food using organic methods and rely on sustainable farming techniques passed down through generations.
    - **Relevance**: These communities serve as the backbone of Amish gardening traditions, where farming and gardening are integral to the Amish way of life.

Historical References: How Amish Farming Has Evolved Over the Centuries

1. **"The Amish in the American Landscape" by David L. McConnell**
    - **Overview**: This book offers a historical account of Amish life, including the development of farming practices. It traces how the Amish adapted to American agricultural landscapes and how their farming methods evolved as they moved from Europe to North America.
    - **Relevance**: A key text for understanding the historical evolution of Amish farming, including how the

community adapted its agricultural practices to new conditions in America.
2. **"Amish Agriculture and Rural Life" by John A. Hostetler**
    - **Overview**: A classic text exploring how Amish farming has developed in North America. Hostetler examines how the Amish, despite modern pressures, have preserved their agricultural traditions and adapted their farming techniques over time.
    - **Relevance**: Offers historical context for Amish farming and gardening, showing how these practices have evolved while maintaining a commitment to self-sufficiency and sustainability.
3. **"The Evolution of Amish Farming in North America" by Donald B. Kraybill**
    - **Overview**: Kraybill, an expert on Amish culture, explores how Amish farming practices have evolved in response to technological changes and external economic pressures. He looks at how Amish communities balance tradition with innovation in their agricultural practices.
    - **Relevance**: This work is invaluable for understanding the changes Amish farming has undergone, particularly in terms of sustainability and adaptation in a modern world.
4. **"Amish Roots: A Living History" by Emma Byler**
    - **Overview**: A historical exploration of Amish farming and gardening traditions, including early farming practices brought over from Europe and how these have been refined and adapted in North America over centuries.
    - **Relevance**: Provides a broader historical context for understanding Amish farming and gardening traditions, including the importance of maintaining these practices for future generations.

Conclusion

The Amish have cultivated a rich tradition of sustainable gardening and farming that continues to inspire people around the world today. By reading these books and resources, you can gain a deeper understanding of Amish gardening techniques, their historical roots, and how their farming practices have evolved over the centuries. Whether you are interested in heirloom gardening, organic practices, or self-sufficiency, these resources will provide valuable insights and practical knowledge to help you replicate Amish-inspired gardening practices in your own life.

The Amish approach to gardening and farming is deeply intertwined with their culture, beliefs, and values, and by exploring these resources, you can learn how their methods contribute to sustainable living and food security.

About the Author

Bradford M. Smith, born 1967 and raised in Lancaster County, PA, has been a polymath when it comes to life. Brad's interests range widely across business, philosophy, science, cooking, travel, magic, the arts, spirituality, engineering, mystery, fantasy, writing, psychology, wellness, sports and history.

After attending Shippensburg University for Accounting and Marketing, Brad started several independent businesses and organizations in the construction and advertising industries prior to focusing on the global franchise industry over 25 years ago with a love of small business and entrepreneurship.

When not writing, speaking, awarding franchises, consulting or just dwelling in thought, Brad enjoys the outdoors, nature, gardening, family, and the occasional cigar, while living with his wife, Judy, in West Palm Beach, FL.